The East Bay Out

OTHER BOOKS BY MALCOLM MARGOLIN

The Earth Manual:
How to Work on Wild Land Without Taming It

The Ohlone Way:
Indian Life in the San Francisco-Monterey Bay Area

The Way We Lived:
California Indian Reminiscences,
Stories, and Songs

The East Bay Out

A PERSONAL GUIDE TO
THE EAST BAY REGIONAL PARKS

by Malcolm Margolin

Illustrations by Carl Dennis Buell
Maps by Sharon G. Johnson

HEYDAY BOOKS, BERKELEY, CALIFORNIA

Editing: Rina Margolin
Illustrations: Carl Dennis Buell
Cartography: Sharon G. Johnson
Design: Sarah Levin
Production Management: Joyce Jenkins
Copy-editing: Julie Trosper
Typesetting: Archetype, Berkeley
Map compositing: Litholab, Berkeley

Published by Heyday Books
P. O. Box 9145 Berkeley, CA 94709

Published with the cooperation of the East Bay
Regional Park District, 11500 Skyline Blvd.,
Oakland, CA 94619.

ISBN: 0-930588-15-0 (paperback)
ISBN: 0-930588-35-5 (clothbound)

10   9   8   7   6   5   4   3   2   1

Acknowledgments

I am grateful, first and foremost, to my wife, Rina Margolin, for editing and partnership—especially for continually sending me back to the typewriter despite my insistence that every draft was perfect. Many of the best phrases in this book are hers.

Sharon Johnson, Carl Buell, and Sarah Levin have shown the generosity of time and spirit that have pushed the maps, illustrations, and design beyond the competent into the truly beautiful. I feel honored by their efforts.

I am also very grateful to the East Bay Regional Park District for the grant that made this updated and expanded edition possible, and for their extraordinary kindliness when the manuscript was one year, two years, three years, and finally nearly four years late. Thanks to Mary Jefferds, Harlan Kessel, and Lynn Bowers of the Board of Directors. And special thanks to Nancy McKay of the Park District's public affairs department and to Jerry Kent, the assistant general manager, for being unfailingly helpful over the years.

I also greatly appreciate the efforts of Julie Trosper who copy-edited the manuscript, Jannie Dresser who typeset it, Jean Ann Carroll who helped prepare the map contours, Dan Gottlieb who orchestrated the camera work on the maps, Joyce Jenkins who proofread and helped manage the production of the book, and Genevieve Fong, Lisa Orlando, Tom Traub, Elizabeth Weiss, Beth Stone, and countless others who provided help in various ways.

And I am still grateful to those who, back in 1974, helped with the first edition of this book: Larry DiStasi, Nancy Clement, Barbara Bash, Hal Hershey, Monte Monteagle, Kent Watson, Dave Hupp, Dick Raymond, Strawdog, Clifford Burke, Scott Swanton, Pete Wickware, Ron Russo, and Tim Gordon. And, although never adequately expressed, I think often of the debt I owe to Guido, Greg Phillips, Bob Blau, and the late Bob Savatone for hiring me at Redwood Regional Park in the early

1970s and creating a work environment that allowed people like me to flourish.

Finally, I am thankful beyond measure to my children, Reuben, Sadie, and Jacob, and to my parents, Max and Rose Margolin, for their warmth and support, and for making me a link in the chain of life. To them I can do no less than dedicate this book.

Contents

Maps

Introduction

The East Bay Regional Park District operates more than forty parks scattered throughout Alameda and Contra Costa counties. They include eight freshwater lakes, two islands (one in the Bay, the other in the Delta), three family campgrounds, and over a thousand miles of hiking trails. Within these parks you can find oak woodlands, pine woodlands, and even a redwood forest. On a given day you can drive to a well-appointed picnic area with cool green lawns and a childrens' playground, or you can hike across ten miles of roadless wilderness to lofty Rose Peak, only thirty-two feet lower than Mount Diablo. The forty miles of bayshore managed by the East Bay Regional Park District include saltwater marshes, mudflats, sandy beaches, fishing piers, salt evaporating ponds, and rocky breakwaters, each with its own mood, tone, wildlife, and recreational possibilities. In Fremont, you can visit a nineteenth century farm where draft horses still plow fields of wheat; or you can stop at a reconstructed Ohlone Indian village, where naturalists and volunteers build boats out of tule, chip arrowheads out of obsidian, start fire with sticks, and twist milkweed fiber into strong, usable string.

It has been primarily through the 60,000 acres of East Bay Regional Park District land—over ninety square miles altogether—that I have come to appreciate the beauty and history of the East Bay. I visit the bayshore parks each fall to observe the grand migration of geese and ducks, long lines of them pouring down the Pacific Flyway from Alaska, Canada, and even Siberia. I hike through the snow that powders the highest peaks each winter, and I watch the greening of the grasses and the rebirth of hundreds of creeks, brooks, and rills in the meadows below. I wander along ridgetops where fossil clamshells remind me, gently but insistently, that there existed worlds of beauty and complexity here long before ours, and that there will be many such worlds long after ours is gone. Each spring I witness the burst of leaf-buds on the trees, the explosion of wildflowers on the meadows, and the return of songbirds from Central America—predictable, I suppose, but always coming as such a surprise that every year I hear myself saying, "I have never seen a spring as lovely as this."

When I first visited the East Bay in 1968, the beauty and scale of these parklands came as an unexpected delight. My friend from college days, David Nawi, took me for a walk from his home in the Berkeley flatlands to Tilden Park. We sat on a ridgetop looking out over miles of valleys and mountains, meadows, and forests. A deer grazed in the shade of a large oak, no more than a hundred feet from us. I was stunned that such excess of beauty existed anywhere in the world, let alone within walking distance of a city like Berkeley.

I have been visiting these parks for nearly twenty years. I have collected apples each year from the same wild apple tree and sought out the same sheltered slope where Douglas irises grow. As the Park District has acquired new land—nearly tripling its size in the dozen or so years since I wrote the first edition of this book—I have extended my wanderings. Yet despite so many years of increasing familiarity with the East Bay landscape, I still find myself as surprised and delighted by the excess of beauty as I was that first day in Tilden.

Further Information

The East Bay Regional Park District has an excellent and responsive Public Affairs Department that provides maps and publications and can answer almost any question about the parks. Call them at (415) 531–9300. Swimming hours, fishing regulations, access for the handicapped, naturalist programs, and trails open to mountain bikes are examples of areas where specific and up-to-date information is available.

For information on public transportation to the parks, it would be best to call AC Transit (839–2882) or BART (465–2278). Picnic sites and campsites for organized groups may be reserved by calling the Park District's reservation office at 531–9043.

HILLS

 For those of us living in the flatlands of the East Bay, the hills that rise up behind us are like a theatrical backdrop. Long ago when tiny bands of Ohlone Indians were collecting shellfish from the Bay, or when the Spanish first settled here on their sprawling *ranchos,* this backdrop of meadows and forests was appropriate to the pastoral dramas being played on the broad stage of the flatlands.

But cities grew along the shores of the Bay. They became bigger, denser, more exciting, and more frantic, until today most of us are actors in an immensely complicated play we can't begin to understand. The lovely backdrop of the hills seems almost out of place against our modern cities. Indeed, there are real estate developers who would like nothing better than to decorate it with houses and roads—a scenery more in line with the current performance.

Fortunately, the real estate developers have not succeeded. And on warm summer mornings, on clear winter afternoons, on spring weekends, some of us escape from the stage, shake off our roles, tell the crazy producers and directors that we've had it up to here; and we climb into that backdrop, into the folds and ridges of the scenic curtain, through its meadows and its forests, into the land of the Ohlones, high up into the hills, where we find. . . .

Bishop Ranch

Bishop Ranch Regional Open Space lies at the edge of a suburban development in the southern part of the San Ramon Valley. It is a relatively small park, some 372 acres of oak woodland and open meadows. By hiking at a steady pace you can cover its entire trail system in well under two hours. Yet I have spent days among its oak groves, returning again and again to watch the pale yellow-green flowers cascade out of the valley oaks in the spring, the acorns swell and ripen on the live oaks throughout the summer, and the leaves of the black oaks burst into flame each fall. As I wander beneath the branches and around the trunks of these trees, I often have a vague, haunting sense that I am searching for something lost—something lost so long ago that I am no longer quite certain what it is, let alone where to find it.

At least the "something lost" is not the trail. Bishop Ranch has a well-marked footpath that leads from the staging area through an open oak woodland up to a grassy ridgetop. A broad fire trail runs along the ridgetop, and from here you can drop down into a quiet, sheltered valley nestled between this ridge and the bold, massive Las Trampas Ridge to the west. In so small a park, it would take some truly world-class absent-mindedness to get seriously lost.

The "something lost" that I am searching for at Bishop Ranch is far more elusive than a footpath. It is a feeling—a feeling that was once the common property of people throughout much of the world, but which has now almost entirely evaporated: a feeling of respect, of intimacy, even of worship that people from earliest times have had for oak groves such as these.

Indian people who walked up these slopes for thousands

of years before the coming of the Spaniards looked at these oaks with deeper affection and (despite important gains in the botanical sciences during the last century) with deeper knowledge as well. Acorns were a mainstay of their diet; the flowering of the oaks and the ripening of the acorns were matters of greatest concern. According to the Indians, acorns did not grow freely, a "wild" food to be plucked at will. Rather, acorns and people were bound together by an ancient compact: only as long as people gave oaks the proper songs, dances, and religious ceremonies would the oaks give people bountiful crops of acorns.

In Europe, as well, oaks dominated not only the forests, but the mythic imagination. To the Greeks, the oak was the "tree of Zeus"; to the Romans, "Jove's own tree"; to the English, the "king of the forest." Oak groves were often held to be sacred, and the very name "druid" is thought to have derived from *deru,* the Celtic word for oak. In the days, not really so long ago, when Europeans were bands of tribal people in the great European forests, oaks were their cathedrals and their castles: history was marked everywhere by particular oaks under whose branches treaties, meetings, battles, coronations, and other momentous events had taken place.

With such thoughts in mind, I come to hike in Bishop Ranch. A modern man, I am clumsy and self-conscious when it comes to practicing outright tree-worship. But I resolve to do what I can, to give to the oaks around me the homage I can legitimately give: close observation, respectful appreciation, and perhaps gratitude to these fine trees for having supported our species so well in earlier ages.

From the staging area, the Grey Fox Trail crosses a creek and winds upslope through a grove of valley oaks. On the lower part of the slope, the valley oaks (*Quercus lobata*) are close together, rather dwarfed, perhaps hybrids. Further up, they are spaced more widely and grow increasingly larger. By midslope, one comes upon some truly stately specimens. In full form the valley oak is so much like the classic European oak (*Quercus robor*) that the Spanish named it *roble* after the tree of their native land, and one can easily see why.

I was once standing beneath one of these great trees with my youngest son, Jakie, who was then five. We looked up into the branches for a while, lost in our thoughts. Then each of us spoke. "What a great tree to climb," said Jakie enthusiastically. "What a great place to lie down," I said at the same time. We laughed at each other, I accusing him of wanting to be a squirrel, he accusing me of wanting to take a nap. We then made an agreement: if he would lie down for a while beneath the tree with me, I would climb up into its branches with him.

Lying below, one becomes fully aware of the wonderful shape of the valley oak. From the main trunk, branches arc upwards in massive, graceful curves, much like the branches of an elm. From these great, arching limbs, other branches—gnarled, with multiple elbows—reach outward, inward, and even downward to fill out the form. A fully developed valley oak reaches yet another stage of growth, the so-called "weeping" stage, when whip-like shoots shower down from the branches almost to the ground to complete its grandeur. From below we can see that this tree, as massive as it is, is still only at the edge of such maturity.

"Come back to visit this tree when you are an old man," I say to Jakie.

Jakie looks puzzled. "Let's climb, daddy," he says, as if to correct me.

We clamber through the sun-dappled branches, among the leaves with their deep, rounded lobes; among the large, long acorns; among the oak galls which hang like Christmas ornaments. The bark of the trunk and larger branches is whitish gray with deep vertical furrows and horizontal cracks that create a rectangular pattern. Crusty lichens and beds of thick moss cover parts of the trunk. On the ends of stubby twigs we find jewelled collars of insect eggs, amber and glistening. A spider plucks at the strings of its web. Swallows swoop close to the tree to snap at insects. We watch a lizard skitter along a gnarled limb and disappear into a deep furrow of the bark. The lizard has lived on this tree all of its life, I suspect. This tree is its entire world, its entire universe, and it seems to me that a tree such as this is indeed universe enough.

Further up the slope the valley oaks become mixed with the coast live oaks (*Quercus agrifolia*). Called *encina* by the Spaniards, this tree, with its stiff, spiny, variable, holly-like leaves, is the most familiar of all Bay Area trees, the oak for which Oakland was named. The sight of a live oak on a hillside, with its smoky gray bark, its short trunk, its exaggerated lean to one side, and its thick rounded crown—this, more than any other single image, symbolizes the East Bay landscape for me.

Here at Bishop Ranch, while common enough, the live oak is hardly dominant. Probably it is too far from the coast. But, as if in compensation, the live oaks here are free from crowding by members of their own species. Widely spaced, they seem to have developed fuller crowns and even more complex characters than usual. Their acorns are small, but often plentiful, and as I look at the stiff, waxy leaves I wonder how many lifetimes it would take to count the number of leaves on a single tree. I study the shapes of these leaves, and wonder if—after a lifetime of counting their number—one could find even two leaves that were identical in size and shape.

Higher up on the slope, to the north of the trail, is a grove of still another species of oak, the black oak (*Quercus kelloggii*). Somewhat uncommon in the Bay Area, this tree generally grows in the high Sierra and Coast Ranges at elevations of 2,000 to 7,000 feet. For me the most stunning aspect of this tree is its leaves—broad, deeply lobed, jagged, and tipped with bristles. These leaves have the most delicate pink tinge to them when they first burst out of their bud cases in the early spring. Then they become black and glistening, so that even on the hot dry days of late spring they look freshly washed and polished. As summer progresses they lose some of their luster, becoming increasingly worn and full of holes from insect attacks, until fall when they suddenly flare up with an intense yellow flame before dropping to the ground. It is generally said that the black oak is named for its charcoal gray trunk—certainly a striking feature—but I sometimes wonder if it is not also named for the black, almost liquid pool of shade its leaves cast even on the hottest summer days.

The acorns of the black oak, huge and bitter, were a favorite of the local Indians. Today they are left largely to the squirrels, who can be seen in the branches, showing off their glorious, twitching tails. Sometimes they curve their tails high above them, like tightrope walkers holding an umbrella for balance. Other times they pull them behind like streamers as they leap from branch to branch in the grove of black oaks. With the local Indians mostly gone and the European druids but a memory, these squirrels—I think to myself—are the resident high priests of the oak grove.

Once you reach the open meadows at the top of the ridge, you can choose between two quite different valleys. On one hand, you can drop down into the small, unnamed valley to the west. A creek runs through it, and the valley is shaded by sycamores, bays, and big-leaf maples. It is a gentle valley, innocent and intimate, its air poignantly sweet, its silence (except for the occasional squabbling of jays) lush and sensual. Here you will find an almost pristine example of the California *pastoral,* the place people have dreamed about for the last hundred years whenever they dreamed of California.

On the other hand, you can pause at the ridgetop and look eastward at another valley, the San Ramon Valley. The clusters of tract homes and shopping centers, the industrial complexes that look like immense Neapolitan wafers, the dull roar of freeway traffic—all this is painfully present. Yet even in the midst of such overdevelopment, there remains enough of the natural world in the San Ramon Valley to suggest a time when this, too, was the essence of the California *pastoral*. In a bygone age, the Franciscan *padres* of Mission San Jose in Fremont used to send flocks of Mission sheep to graze on the tall grasses of this fertile, well-watered dell. The man who tended the sheep was named Ramon, and in Spanish times the valley came to be called "Ramon's Valley." Later Anglo residents added the title "San" to his name to give their valley a more "authentic" Spanish sound. In so informal a manner, did a sheepherder named Ramon join Peter, Paul, Luke, and the assemblage of other saints.

As I walk back down the slope to the staging area, I cannot help but think of Ramon. How little he would comprehend the developments and the people who now inhabit the valley that bears his name! How amazed—and surely uncomfortable—he would be to hear these strange people referring to him as a saint! But (I think) this is surely nonsense. For if Ramon were to return with his flock of sheep he would hardly be wandering, lost and confused, among the tract homes and the shopping malls; rather, he would, like me, be found under these oaks, moving slowly—very slowly—absorbing the peacefulness and wisdom of land that has scarcely changed since Mission days.

Directions: From Highway 680, between Danville and Dublin, take the Crow Canyon Rd. exit. Head west to San Ramon Valley Blvd. (the first traffic light), and turn left. Head south along San Ramon Valley Blvd. approximately two miles to Morgan Dr. Turn right on Morgan Dr. and continue about four blocks to the park entrance.

Briones

Briones Regional Park is a 5,300-acre semi-wilderness area that lies between Lafayette and Martinez. It is an area of high bucking hills, broad valleys, creeks, meadows, ponds, waterfalls, and forests. This is a park primarily for hikers, and the hiking is splendid. The hills have a glorious, windy, high-country feeling to them—the sort of wild feeling that makes you want to break loose and run like a joyous crazy down the rippling meadows. The valleys (Abrigo, Homestead, Willow Flat, and Bear Creek) are wide, motherly valleys that gurgle with springs and song birds. Cattle graze on the meadows, deer browse at the edges of the woods, and hawks play with the breezes overhead. People stop to picnic, often in the shade of a massive valley oak, and even those who have never so much as planted a radish seed begin to daydream about owning a farm in a place "just like this."

Briones is a park where, especially on overcast days, you are likely to see more deer than hikers. Deer are everywhere. They push their long, gentle faces into the cool grass of the meadows. They munch acorns thoughtfully at the edges of the forests. They cluster together in small clearings as if posing for a family portrait. Keep a sharp eye out, and sticking out of the brush you will probably see those erect ears, tensed bodies, frozen faces, and big unblinking eyes that watch your every move. Maintain a polite distance and they continue to stare at you. Edge closer and they trot gracefully away. But move toward them suddenly and they boing-boing-boing away into the nearest thicket as if on pogo sticks.

While deer are always timid, the cattle here seem at first to be almost malevolent, especially when a big herd of them is blocking your path. This puts the urban hiker into a dilemma. Should you act the role of a coward and give the cattle wide berth? Or should you plunge right through them, preparing to execute a half-veronica in the style of Juan Belmonte?

If you find yourself with this problem, be assured that the Herefords, the brown cattle with the white faces, are very docile. The black cattle are Angus. While Angus bulls are supposed to be testy, the young steers and heifers at Briones are far from dangerous. So walk resolutely toward them and the herd of baleful-looking beasts will obligingly scatter before you.

But what are cattle doing in this semi-wilderness park in the first place? Don't they trample the wildflowers, compete with the deer, and totally upset the balance of nature? Wouldn't Briones be better off without them?

The truth is that rather than being intruders, cattle are actually the creators of the East Bay grassland environment. When the Spanish first arrived some two centuries ago, the meadowlands of this area were covered with perennial grasses—the so-called "bunch grasses" with long, tough roots and an ability to survive the summer's heat. The Spanish lost no time in introducing cattle. Tangled in the hair of the cattle were the seeds of the European grasses—grasses that die back each summer and grow again from seed in the fall, grasses that eventually were to take over the East Bay meadowlands almost completely.

By changing the grasslands of the East Bay, cattle may have created a permanent niche for themselves here, especially in the drier, inland areas like Briones. Without their grazing, the annual grasses would grow waist-high, die back in the summer, and become a major fire hazard. Also, cattle are valuable for browsing on brush which might otherwise invade the fields of comparatively weak-rooted annual grasses. The one major drawback of cattle is that by disturbing the soil, they often encourage the growth of thistles, much in evidence in parts of Briones.

Except for the change in the grasslands, however, Briones seems to be quite unspoiled. I doubt that the mosaic of dense forests and open meadows has changed much since 1829 when Felipe Briones, a retired Spanish soldier, fell in love with a waterfall and decided to settle upon the land. He lived here for a decade, supporting his family of eighteen. But in 1839 a band of Indians stole horses from his neighbor, Ygnacio Martinez. Felipe Briones, the ex-soldier, was called upon to help recover the horses. In the battle which followed he was struck by an arrow and killed. After his death his widow, Dona Maria Manuela Valencia de Briones, received title to 13,353 acres (over twenty square miles), of which Briones Regional Park covers only a small part. Most of the rest of this once vast *rancho* has been acquired by the East Bay Municipal Utility District as part of the San Pablo Reservoir watershed.

Those of us who know Briones well feel that this is one of the most exciting places in the East Bay. It is an undeveloped park with lots of space. Hikers along Briones Crest enjoy splendid views of the Bay, Mount Diablo, and (on clear days) the Sierra in the distance.

I visit Briones often, but my favorite time of year is fall when this big park first shakes off its summer sleep. As the days get cooler and shorter, certain trees (most notably the big-leaf maples) turn fall colors. The thick forests of Briones become dappled with yellows, browns, and russets. Leaves of the climbing grape vines shoot bold touches of red throughout the trees. Hear ye, hear ye, all you displaced New Englanders! There is a rich and colorful autumn to be found in the woodlands of Briones.

The second great autumn change in Briones comes with the first rains. All summer the meadows lay dry and golden, a slumbering giant. With the first rains the giant awakens. Millions of grass seeds burst open, and waves of green wash over the golden hills.

Newts are among the first to celebrate. After the first heavy rains thousands and thousands of these orange-bellied, brown-backed creatures appear throughout Briones as if by spontaneous generation. On cool, rainy fall days it's hard to find a square yard of grassland or forest that doesn't have its own resident newt. They have the same shape as lizards, but totally different personalities. Lizards are sunshine creatures, light and fast. Newts, on the other hand, are creatures of moist, dank places. They are stiff and sluggish, with cold rubbery skin. They act as if they had just crawled out of the refrigerator and haven't quite warmed up yet. You can easily pick one up, handle it, and put it down. Rub its back lightly and it will go into a "defensive position." It is a minor miracle that such a sluggish creature ever catches anything to eat.

By late autumn the ponds and lagoons in the hills fill once again with water. Freshwater ponds are rare in the Bay Area, so be sure to enjoy them while you're here. Peer into one of these ponds and you will see schools of tiny fish shimmering this way and that. Frogs croak at each other with unabashed machismo. Freshwater snails meticulous-

ly explore the newly submerged grasses.

The creeks of Briones also begin to flow again. In early fall there are only tenuous splatterings and murmurings, but by late winter the creeks become boisterous and high-spirited. Waterfalls splash and dash along Cascade Creek, ferns spill over the banks, and in the dark canyons drops of water glisten like jewels in the green micro-worlds of moss.

By Christmas time the water has won its battle against the summer drought. Elsewhere snow may be falling and icicles forming, but in the East Bay we have every reason to be celebrating the annual miracle of a green Christmas.

By early spring the grasses become tall and loose, waving and rippling sensuously in the meadows. Thousands of sluggish newts now make their way to the ponds for their springtime mating orgy. In the water they take on a new, romantic identity. They tuck their legs in against their bodies, and with a few strong undulations of the tail they propel themselves through the water as quickly and effortlessly as fish. By late March the newts disappear entirely and the meadows are dotted with wildflowers. Then the grass bolts to seed, and the land prepares itself once again for the hot dry summer.

To me Briones has always been charming, but I remember one day in particular when the land seemed to reach out to me and become almost excruciatingly alive. I was hiking along, rucksack on my back, thoughtless and casual, when I heard a very distant, mournful, whistling sound. It was an eerie, monotonous song, and every so often the pitch would change. It seemed to be coming from everywhere at once.

For a long time this hollow, haunting song followed me along the trail. Were there Sirens here such as sang to Ulysses and his men? Was it the keening of the widow Briones for her dead husband? Was it the singing of a Saclan Indian for his lost land, his lost language? Was it the song of the land itself?

I found this distant whistling to be infinitely sad and

infinitely beautiful. It was the song of the trees, the grasses, the soil, and all the strange, beautiful, and tragic people who once lived here. It was a simple song that flowed through the branches of the oaks, around the high peaks, between the blades of grass, back through the past and out into the future, through my mind and beyond—a lonesome, lovely song that was wrapping everything together in a thin, strong blanket of sound.

I feel almost foolish telling you how the song ended. I reached into my rucksack for my canteen. When I turned the cap of the canteen the song popped and abruptly ceased. It had been air seeping through a narrow opening of the canteen cap. I felt slightly chagrined, but still elated. The singer may have been a faulty canteen cap. But what remains with me is the feeling of enchantment that the song had drawn out of the land and laid before me like a precious gift—an enchantment that is a real and rightful part of Briones Park.

Directions: To reach the Bear Creek entrance to Briones from Oakland, take Highway 24 east through the Caldecott Tunnel to the Orinda exit. Turn left (north) onto Camino Pablo, which becomes San Pablo Dam Rd. Continue north to Bear Creek Rd., then turn right. Pass the Briones Reservoir and the intersection with Happy Valley Rd., then turn right at the sign into Briones.

To reach the remaining entrances from Oakland, take Highway 24 (east) through the Caldecott Tunnel to the Pleasant Hill Rd. off ramp. Follow Pleasant Hill Rd. north a short distance to the Lafayette Ridge Staging Area, just past Acalanes High School. Lafayette Ridge Trail heads west into the park. To the east is the new Briones-Mount Diablo Trail which travels 11.5 miles through public and private lands to Mount Diablo State Park. Maps are available from the East Bay Regional Park District or at the trail head.

Further along Pleasant Valley Rd.—shortly after its junction with Spring Hill Rd.—bear left on to Reliez Valley Rd. Follow it north to reach the other entrances to Briones.

See Map C.

Anthony Chabot

Anthony Chabot Regional Park is a huge, 4,700-acre park in the hills above East Oakland and San Leandro. It has vast areas of grassland, brush, oak-bay forests, eucalyptus forests, and even a stand of redwoods—all spread out in a leisurely, generous fashion and crisscrossed by a few wide fire trails. A very few fire trails, in fact. Much of Anthony Chabot has no trails at all. The grasslands and the more open forests are yours to wander over, but the dense brushland is almost totally inaccessible to anyone larger than a fox or a brush rabbit. This impenetrable brush is the last true wilderness remaining in the city of Oakland.

Throughout this sprawling land are scattered a number of "attractions": picnic areas, group camping areas, a family campground (see page 189), a rifle range, an archery range, the 315-acre Lake Chabot (see page 150), an equestrian center, and a golf course.

But despite the hodgepodge of attractions, Anthony Chabot has a peculiar quietness of its own. It has many exquisite nooks and canyons where you can hide from the twentieth century. My favorite is Bird Trail, a mile-long, very narrow, intimate loop trail that runs off MacDonald Trail near MacDonald Gate. The trail follows a bouncing creek, and it is a botanical museum of rare and beautiful plants. Perhaps I am particularly fond of this trail since I helped build it when I worked for the Park District in the early 1970s.

Another private nook is Buckeye Canyon, a small box canyon whose entrance is behind the row of eucalyptus trees at the north end of Bort Meadow. Buckeye Canyon is Irish-green in the early spring with its growth of glistening mosses and ferns. If you poke around you may find the remains of an old cistern that supplied water to a ranch that stood here during the last century.

There are other hidden corners in Anthony Chabot, and if you spend a few days wandering around you'll surely discover more of your own. But I cannot pretend that Anthony Chabot as a whole is a truly spectacular park. It doesn't reach out and entice you with its prettiness the way some of the lakes do, nor does it overwhelm you with its grandeur. The scenery here is understated. I know it's iconoclastic for me to admit this—we nature lovers are supposed to be in a constant state of ecstasy, alive at every pore, vibrating like bees—but one day I even found myself *bored*. I had been to Anthony Chabot dozens of times, and the park had become for me as stale as old beer, when I turned a corner and noticed a fox sitting in the trail. The fox got up and walked ahead of me, imitating my dispirited shuffle, throwing occasional glances back at me to make sure I was watching. I stopped in amazement. The fox lay down in the middle of the trail, curled up its body, nestled its nose into its tail, and looked at me with pitying eyes. When I moved closer the fox reluctantly arose, moved on a few more yards, and curled up again to look at me some more. Then suddenly it disappeared into the brush. The trail was empty again, but a feeling of cleanness and newness swept over me that I cannot explain. I had seen many foxes before, but this was the first fox I had ever really *seen*.

In some ways Anthony Chabot has become for me like a modest theater I used to go to. The staging, the acoustics, and the seating were all rather ordinary. But it was here that I saw some of the most exciting plays I've ever seen. That's how it's been with Anthony Chabot. Here, more than anywhere else, I have had the experience of cracking through what I've been programmed to see and catching a glimpse of the world beyond. It happened at the unexpected sight of a flower that seemed to cut into me so deeply I got scared; in a vulture's mid-flight wobble that seemed to last forever; in the plunge of a hawk so precipitous that the bottom seemed to have fallen out of the earth;

and in the curious wrap-around and swish of the fox's tail as he stared at me with pitying eyes. There were times at Anthony Chabot when the murkiness of ordinary perception lifted and I felt that I could see things directly, immediately—as they really are.

But whatever I might think of Anthony Chabot at present, I know that if I return in another twenty or thirty years I'll have to revise my opinion. Anthony Chabot is undergoing a profound ecological change. It had always been predominantly grassland. Aerial photos from before 1942 (when the Park District acquired the land) show vast areas of grass and only about 275 acres of brush in the whole park. Twenty years later, in 1963, another survey found the grassland disappearing and there were then 750 acres of brush. Brush has been creeping over "Grass Valley" (as this area was once called) at the rate of nearly twenty-five acres a year. (Similar invasions are taking place at Redwood Park and Tilden.)

Many theories exist to explain why the brush is taking over. Some say it's because grazing was excluded for many years, and cattle would have tended to trample and browse the young brush—so in recent years cattle have been reintroduced. Others feel it's because fire has been over-controlled, and the grasslands need periodic burning to keep them grassy. Still others conjecture that the basic cause is the change of grasses in this area: European annual grasses have replaced the deep-rooted native perennials which might have held the land better. Most likely all of these factors play some part.

Also, the species of brush leading the invasion, coyote brush, is admirably equipped to take over the meadows. A relative of the aster, coyote brush has composite flowers—the latest, most improved invention of the plant kingdom. Its seeds are numerous and float great distances on little parachutes. If you dig up a coyote brush you'll see that its roots are extensive and greedy, often three times as deep as the plant is tall. Rub your fingers over the leaf, and you'll feel a waxy covering, cutin, that protects the leaf by pre-

venting the hot sun from burning the tender cells deeper within.

Some ecologists and recreation administrators bemoan the loss of meadowland. And with good reason. Meadows are a lot more fun to look at and play on than brush. They also support more wildflowers. Nevertheless, the brush environment is not without its virtues. It provides food and shelter for innumerable small animals and birds; and the current mixture of grass, brush, and forest at Anthony Chabot is probably the best possible environment for wildlife.

But even the victory of the brush is only a temporary victory. Built into the marvellous mechanisms of the coyote brush is a tragic flaw: as the patches of brush get thicker and thicker, denser and denser, they shade the ground below them more and more. Within this shade no other coyote brush can grow: the filtered sunlight is not strong enough to penetrate the thick cutinous layer of wax on the leaves. But the seedlings of other plants are better adapted to the shade. Within the older stands of coyote brush you can often see elderberry, oak, bay, madrone, and the other trees and bushes that will make up the hardwood forests of the future. In another hundred years people may wonder why in the world this forested area was ever called "Grass Valley."

Directions: From Oakland and Berkeley take Highway 13 (the Warren Freeway) to the Redwood Rd. exit. Head east (toward the hills) on Redwood Rd. to Skyline Blvd. To reach the MacDonald Gate, Bort Meadow, Marcial Gate, or Willow Park entrances, continue along Redwood Rd. To reach the equestrian center or the Grass Valley Rd. entrance, turn right (south) on Skyline Blvd.
See Map D.

Claremont Canyon

Claremont Canyon Regional Preserve covers some two hundred acres in the Berkeley Hills, most of them very steep. Along with the adjacent Strawberry Canyon Preserve owned by the University of California, this is the big, open land of untamed meadows and dark forests that rises so fetchingly above the flatlands of Berkeley. Whenever I look east from my home or office, this land beckons, reminding me that foxes, wildflowers, brush rabbits, and deer can be found within a twenty minute walk. And many times—I am proud to admit—I heed the beckoning; I leave the half-written chapters, the unanswered letters, and all the unsolved problems behind, mumble something about an "important meeting," and—as they used to say in the old westerns—head for the hills.

My route to Claremont Canyon Preserve takes me through tree-lined streets and past elegant brown-shingle homes. Wisteria cascades from trellises over their entranceways. Front lawns are landscaped with roses, camellias, hydrangeas, hibiscus, and other exotic and highly cultivated flowers from around the world. Lawn sprinklers send gentle fantasies of spray into the air.

My walk eventually brings me through the grounds of the old School for the Blind and Deaf, a collection of Spanish-style buildings that now serve as University dorms. At the southwest corner of this site, a fire road rises steeply through a cool, medicinal-smelling grove of eucalyptus, then breaks into the open brush and meadowland of Claremont Canyon Preserve.

After the lush landscaping of the well-to-do neighborhoods below, the vegetation in the Preserve at first seems scruffy and relatively colorless. The wildflowers, unlike the cultivars below, are simple in form and for the most part scattered widely, sometimes inconspicuously, among unruly grasses that bolt to seed in late spring and turn tawny brown in summer. If I were coming here simply to please the eye with beautiful plants, I would have been just as well off wandering the residential streets of Berkeley. What brings me here, however, is a longing for what cultivated gardens cannot provide: spaciousness, freedom to wander, relative solitude, and most of all the experience of an environment not created and controlled by people. I have come to search out a place where flowers are not our servants, where people are merely guests.

After the steep climb to the ridgetops of Claremont Canyon Preserve, I pause, catch my breath, and turn to scan the meadows and brushland around me. I always find the grasses on this west-facing slope to be a revelation. Touched by the afternoon sun, moistened by summer fogs, and ungrazed for generations, they form thick, luxuriant mats. Lupines and poppies produce the bold patches of blue and gold that once covered all the Berkeley Hills and gave the University its school colors. I find other spring favorites: mule ears (a kind of wild sunflower), soap root, blue dicks, buttercups, blue-eyed grass (a member of the iris family), filaree, vetch (wild sweetpea), mustard, mints, and pimpernel. Even in mid-July, when the inland hills and valleys are dry and dormant, wildflowers still dot these fog-cooled slopes. Sticky monkeyflower, in particular, blooms in abundance, mixing with the green-leafed coyote brush to give the brushlands a rich yellow-and-green pattern.

The vegetation of Claremont Canyon Preserve is familiarly "East Bay." Yet it also has a coastal feeling to it. This, I think, is the kind of vegetation I might find on the Marin Headlands, say, or above the San Mateo beaches. A glance toward the Bay explains why. This ridge lies exactly opposite the Golden Gate; on clear days you can look out into the Pacific Ocean. Ocean breezes and summer fogs enter through the Gate and dash themselves like waves on Claremont Canyon's precipitous slopes. Because of the way this ridge catches the fog, it is much moister and cooler throughout the summer than the hills and valleys a few miles inland, and also far more moderate in temperature during the winter. In fact, Berkeley's temperatures on any given day tend to be much closer to those in Half Moon Bay than to those in Orinda.

I continue through the thick, coarse "coastal" grasses and along the fire trail past the dense stands of brush until I come to a grove of large Monterey pines. In even the lightest breeze their needles stir slightly, shooting rays of silver light into the air. I sit down on a thick bed of pine needles and idly finger a dried twig. The bark crumbles, exposing the inner wood delicately inscribed by insect hieroglyphics. A bird hidden among the branches punctures the air with staccato bursts, as if sending Morse code signals. In the distance I hear intermittent, lazy hammerings, and I am not certain whether it is a woodpecker tapping at a tree or a Sunday carpenter working on the deck of his house.

House! The idea startles me. Why are there no houses here? After all, this area in the Berkeley Hills is, to put it bluntly, highly desirable real estate, and has been so for generations. So where *are* the grand houses with cultivated flower gardens and picture windows overlooking the Bay?

There are, in fact, in Berkeley's City Hall, maps of the area that show Claremont Canyon Preserve looking much like the rest of the Berkeley Hills—chopped up by property lines into rectangular boxes and crisscrossed by streets with expensive-sounding names like "Panoramic Place." This was the so-called "University Uplands" subdivision, created around the turn of the century. Lots in University Uplands (how the real estate interests of the era must have loved that name!) were sold by mail and even door-to-door. Yet the promised streets were never built, the lots never developed. Over the decades ownership passed from hand to hand. In the 1970s, when the East Bay Regional Park District undertook to create Claremont Canyon Regional Preserve, it had to negotiate land purchases with

four hundred separate owners, some of them now scattered widely across the country.

As I wander deeper into what would have been University Uplands, I find, instead of streets, only the slenderest deer trail scratched into the land. I follow it until it stops indeterminately in a tangle of brush, at a spot which the old city map designates as 3751 Panoramic Place. This might have been one of the most prestigious addresses in the Bay Area, the home perhaps of a University professor. But instead of intruding upon a scholar turning the leaves of a book, I hear only a towhee (an overgrown member of the sparrow family) energetically turning dried leaves under a bush, searching (with what eagerness!) for bugs.

A gopher's head protrudes from a hole. "Wonderful view you have," I think, and indeed the view from 3751 Panoramic Place is nothing short of spectacular. Spread out a thousand feet below me is a huge portion of the East Bay shoreline—from Oakland north to Richmond—as well as splendid views of San Francisco Bay. People in the playing field below are tiny, as if seen from an airplane, and the cars on the various bridges are recognizable only as moving glints of light. Ships enter and leave beneath the Golden Gate Bridge, planes line up for the approach to the Oakland Airport. City streets are laid out in straight lines, reminding me of rows of crops on a farm. Freeways, like large, graceful rivers of concrete, curve over the cities. The gopher once again pokes its nose up from the hole. What does the world look like from gopher height, I wonder, and I lay down on the ground to find out. A dark beetle is lumbering along the blades of grass, and from where I am looking a line of cars, mere glints on the Golden Gate Bridge, appears to be draped over its back like a delicate diamond necklace. A blade of grass close to me is bigger than the Transamerica Building. I eye a poppy; this small flower blocks out my view of all of Berkeley.

A single poppy! It is this whimsical and provocative image that I bring back down the trail with me. The image stays with me past the brown-shingle houses and along the tree-lined streets, and I know that it will be around to haunt and delight me for weeks to come.

"Where did you go?" I am asked when I return.

"To visit a friend at 3751 Panoramic Place," I reply with a grin.

Directions: From Ashby Avenue (Highway 13) in Berkeley, turn north on College Ave. After five blocks turn right (east) on Derby St. past the School for the Blind and Deaf site (now the Clark Kerr Campus at the University of California, Berkeley). Park where the flow of traffic turns away from the School. The trail head can be found at the southeast corner of the school grounds, near the beginning of Stonewall Rd.

Garin/Dry Creek Pioneer

From the days of the Spanish Missions to the present, a large part of the East Bay has been ranch land—ranch land on a scale that many counties in Texas or Wyoming can't rival. Over 200,000 acres of Alameda County are currently given over to cattle grazing. Privately-owned ranches still cover hundreds, often thousands of acres each, and in many cases they have been in the same families for generations. Off-limits to hikers and seldom penetrated by public roads, this extensive land tends to be unknown and invisible, even to people living close by. Yet it is this private ranch land, seriously endangered by development, that gives the East Bay much of its rural character, and which—along with areas set aside for parks and watershed—gives mountain lions, eagles, and other wildlife the vast acreage they need to roam, hunt, and reproduce.

Garin Ranch and Dry Creek Pioneer Ranch in the hills above Hayward were formerly two such adjoining private cattle ranches. The East Bay Regional Park District acquired Garin Ranch in the late 1960s, and in 1978 the Meyers sisters, whose family had owned Dry Creek Pioneer Ranch for over a century, donated the 1,200-acre site as a remarkable gift to the Park District.

Together, Garin Ranch and Dry Creek Pioneer Ranch cover some 2,800 acres of meadowland, creeks, and deeply-wooded canyons. A barn at the Garin Avenue entrance serves as a visitors' center, with exhibits and programs on the theme of early California farming. At the southern entrance, the Jordan Pond area is landscaped with a turfed lawn and picnic tables. But except for these minor concessions to interpretation and recreation, the rest of Garin/Dry Creek Pioneer is nothing more than an honest piece of ranch land that has somehow managed to stay out of the way of the twentieth century.

In fact this area feels so authentically like private ranchland that hiking here is almost as good as trespassing. Cattle, after a day of grazing in the high meadows, still plod their way back to the old stock ponds. Corrals and barns are still part of the landscape, and are still used. The hills are as lofty and lovely as they always were, the canyons of willows and sycamores as deep, and the land as generous in its offerings of beauty to anyone who visits.

In the spring wildflowers throw themselves madly over the hills. Flocks of warblers arrive, twinkling among the bushes like Christmas lights. In the shady canyons the buds of the big-leaf maple burst open with a noiseless shower of leaves and blossoms. At night the ground squirrels and rabbits cower in their holes, while foxes prowl through the starry grass and coyotes howl at the moon. In short, what we have here is indeed a rather ordinary, and thereby wonderful, piece of East Bay ranchland.

Much of the wildlife here begins with a tiny plant called filaree. Filaree has a five-petalled, violet flower with a red stem. You may not notice it at first, unless you make a special effort. After a while, though, you'll discover that the grasslands are dotted with these little flowers.

Although the flowers are inconspicuous, filaree seeds have a way of making themselves very well known. At first they look like tiny spears, with pointed heads and more or less straight shafts. But as the humidity changes, different parts of the "shaft" expand and contract at differing rates. The shaft now curls up into a spiral or corkscrew, providing a motion whereby the seed twists itself into the ground—or into one's socks, as every hiker soon discovers.

Not only does filaree turn itself into an amazing seed, but even more incredibly, it can turn itself into a ground squirrel. Filaree is the staff of life for the thousands of these little animals who live here in the Hayward Hills.

Ground squirrels love ranch life and have even prospered with the coming of Europeans. The newcomers plowed up the hard clayey soil and planted wheat and other delicious grains. They also introduced exotic plants, like filaree and like the heavily seeding annual grasses. At the same time the settlers introduced new and delectable foods, they short-sightedly reduced the populations of coyotes, eagles, and other natural predators that had kept the squirrel population within reasonable bounds.

From a fairly insignificant animal among California's fauna, the ground squirrel population burgeoned. They became a major agricultural pest until the 1920s, when the inflated population was hit by plague. Authorities declared them a health hazard. Schools in California were recessed for the day to allow children to get out and kill ground squirrels. Games, competitions, and trophies were organized around the slaughter. Posters were hung in public places, showing President Hoover urging American youth: "Do your patriotic duty. Kill a ground squirrel."

The extermination campaign was disastrous, at least for the people who partook in it. A whole generation was convinced that ground squirrels are dirty, harmful animals. In fact there are still many thousands of people who cannot bring themselves to enjoy these lively, clownish, inquisitive little creatures.

As to whether the campaign had much effect on the ground squirrels, anyone who has ever tried to get rid of mice, rats, or any other rodent knows the answer. Some marginal colonies were destroyed. But by and large the ground squirrels showed such enthusiasm for reproduction that whatever vacancies were created in their ranks were filled quite effortlessly in a few years.

Today the ground squirrel population at Garin/Dry Creek Pioneer is large and prosperous. Squirrels run along their paths, dive into their holes, and return to chirp at an intruder with great gusto. I personally feel that they have a superb sense of humor, but I won't push that point. In any case, they lead public lives and are great fun to watch.

Many predators have been attracted to Garin/Dry Creek Pioneer by the ground squirrels, and paradoxically they benefit the squirrel population by keeping them alert and plague-free. At odd hours you might see a badger here, savagely and single-mindedly excavating a squirrel hole. At dawn or dusk you might happen upon a coyote looking sharply and intelligently over a field before racing off to follow whatever ground squirrel smell is pulling so insistently at its nose. During the day the air is full of hawks swooping low to caress the contours of the hills. Once, after a fire left a ground squirrel colony unusually exposed, as many as eight golden eagles were counted at one time, assembling to share in the easy hunting.

The chain that begins with filaree and ends with coyotes and eagles is only one of the many wildlife chains that run through Garin/Dry Creek Pioneer. Other chains are formed by mice, rabbits, quail, skunks, snakes, raccoons, foxes, and ultimately vultures. Together they make up the thriving wildlife population of a typical East Bay cattle ranch.

By expanding the park area over the last decade, the East Bay Regional Park District has done much to protect this wildlife. But the fight is hardly over. At the current rate of development even this enlarged park will soon be cut off by housing tracts from the wild lands that stretch to the east. If this park does indeed become like an island, what will happen to the wildlife here? I'm not sure. But I hope that wide corridors can be maintained to connect Garin/Dry Creek Pioneer with the rest of the natural world, so that we (and the wildlife) will be spared the pain of having to find out.

Directions: Take Highway 880, the Nimitz Freeway, to Hayward. Exit at Industrial Parkway and head east to Mission Blvd. Turn right (south) on Mission and go about two blocks to Garin Ave. Turn left (east) on Garin Ave. and head about a mile to the park entrance.
See Map G.

Huckleberry Preserve

Huckleberry Botanic Preserve is a unique and distinguished community of plants in the Oakland Hills. Here you will find a dwarf forest of rare shrubs and bushes, and a narrow footpath that threads almost apologetically through the 132-acre preserve.

The land all around Huckleberry Preserve has been altered. It has been planted to Australian blue gum eucalyptus trees, terraced by sheep trails, taken over by European grasses, sectioned off by paved roadways, and dotted by houses. Even the redwoods to the south and west have been logged once, twice, or even three times, and are only now beginning to show off with a hint of their former majesty. But Huckleberry Preserve has never been conquered. Those hardy, scrubby, untamed bushes, as rigid as bone and as alive as fire, are a completely authentic remnant of native California.

Whenever I think of Huckleberry Preserve a very specific scene comes to mind. It is a crisp, clear winter's day, and I am sitting just above the trail. My breath condenses into puffs of smoke. My hands are pushed into my pockets. I am looking at the blue sky through a gnarled, twisted manzanita bush. Its leaves are stiff and waxy, its pink-white flowers dangle like miniature Grecian vases, and its polished red stem is writhing against the sky like a lick of flame. Just then two courting hummingbirds whizz by; they are sparks in the cold winter sky.

But flowers and hummingbirds in the middle of winter? Certainly, for Huckleberry Preseve has a climate of its own. It has something to do with the eastern exposure, the edge of the fog belt, and the mechanics of inversion layering. Here, spring does not wait stubbornly until March or April. It sometimes comes as early as Christmas, and it's

always in full swing by February. On many a gloomy winter's day I've found spring hiding out shyly at the Preserve, and I've hurried back to town with the message to all my house-bound friends: "Spring is alive and well at Huckleberry Preserve." The bell-like manzanita flowers are blooming. On the leatherwood the buds have burst and the lemon-yellow flowers are spilling out. Currants, roses, thimbleberries, and other plants are flowering, and knowledgeable Bay Area hummingbirds have gathered for the magnificent mid-winter bounty.

Huckleberry Preserve is also out of step with the rest of the Bay Area in late summer and early fall. Elsewhere it's hot and dry, and even the most ardent nature lovers usually limit their explorations to the latest issue of *Audubon*. But August through October is nut and berry season at the preserve: huckleberries by the ton, manzanita berries, hazelnuts, chinquapin nuts, silktassel berries, currants, snowberries, nightshade berries—millions of fat berries and nuts that provide a feast for the local birds.

Huckleberry Preserve has also been providing a botanical feast for local naturalists. In 1915 W.L. Jepson, a famous biologist, called this area "inspiring." And botanists have been tramping over Huckleberry Preserve ever since. If you want to find out what excites them so much, here is a sampling:

• Western leatherwood (*Dirca occidentalis*), a plant with pliant, leathery branches that is found only here, a few other places in the East Bay, and nowhere else in the world.

• Huckleberries, so common on the Preserve, but not found anywhere else in the East Bay except in scattered patches near Redwood Peak.

• A manzanita called *Arctostaphylos andersonii* var. *pallida* which grows only in this area and on El Sobrante Ridge.

• Another rare manzanita, *Arctostaphylos crustacea*.

• Silktassel (*Garrya elliptica*), chinquapin, and wild iris, all common on the Preserve, yet fairly rare elsewhere in the East Bay.

• Plus many more bushes, trees, ferns, and flowers. (Many of these plants are marked with numbered posts and described in a pamphlet available at the trail entrance.)

This natural community of rare plants makes Huckleberry Preserve one of the most significant botanical areas in California. But don't let that scare you away. Despite the importance of the place, I must confess that many a plump huckleberry has disappeared down my throat—and (if the truth be known) down the throats of some of California's most illustrious preservationists. Huckleberry Preserve does not have a hushed, don't-touch, museum air about it. The intimate mile-long footpath that passes through the Preserve provides you with a joyous hiking experience. There are views of Flicker Ridge nearby and Las Trampas Ridge to the southeast, while Mount Diablo swells in the distance. And because the foot trail is small, level, and lined with luscious huckleberries it is a very fine trail indeed for little kids. By combining it with a segment of the Skyline Trail just downslope, you can make an easy loop that will take no more than an hour or an hour-and-a-half to hike.

I've visited Huckleberry Preserve perhaps twenty times, and I've developed an extraordinary affection for it. In other East Bay parks I feel dwarfed by the landscape around me. But at Huckleberry Preserve I often feel like a giant striding through a diminutive forest. There is something bracing and energizing about these gnarled, strong bushes, the hardness of their branches, the distinctness and crispness of everything, the unconquered history of the area.

To the Indians the land was full of gods and spirits, and they would go to special mountains, springs, hills, or rivers to court specific types of experiences and powers. Similarly, I visit Huckleberry Preserve for something rarer than a rare shrub—for the feeling of clarity, sharpness, and strength this land can bestow on those who become intimate with it.

Directions: From Highway 13 (the Warren Freeway) take the Joaquin Miller Rd./Lincoln Ave. exit. Head east (toward the hills) along Joaquin Miller Rd. and near the top of the hill turn left onto Skyline Blvd. Follow Skyline past Roberts Recreation Area, the Skyline Gate entrance to Redwood Regional Park, and the intersection of Pinehurst Rd. to the staging area for Huckleberry Preserve. The distance from the intersection of Joaquin Miller Rd. and Skyline Blvd. to the staging area is 4.7 miles.

Kennedy Grove

Kennedy Grove Regional Recreation Area (named in honor of John F. Kennedy) is a small, 95-acre park near the base of the San Pablo Reservoir dam. The main activities here are barbecuing and eating.

With its clustered picnic tables and trimmed lawns Kennedy Grove is very much like a city park. What makes it remarkable, however, are the handsome, young, blue gum eucalyptus trees that shade the picnic areas. These trees were planted by the Water Company in 1910. They are originally from Australia, and like other Australian natives (kangaroos, koala bears, and platypuses) eucalyptus trees are rather strange. They have straight hard trunks, shredding bark, and long curved leaves that smell like Vick's Cough Drops. Branches come crashing to the ground without warning—often on warm, windless summer days.

At the turn of the century eucalyptus was the get-rich-quick tree of California. Millions were planted until the eucalyptus bubble burst in 1911, leaving 50,000 acres of exotic Australian trees to fend for themselves in the California environment. (For more on the history of the East Bay eucalyptus boom, see page 68-71).

How has California wildlife adapted to this strange, new environment? "Badly," claim many experts. Early in my California education it was explained to me that eucalyptus forests are "wildlife deserts." So for many years I hiked through these forests quickly, because obviously there was nothing to see. And sure enough, I saw nothing. The less I saw the more I hurried, the more I hurried the less I saw, until after a while I found that I too could verify the "wildlife desert" theory from my own experience.

One day I was expounding the fine points of this theory

to a naturalist friend of mine. And to my utter amazement my friend began to speak heresies. He talked about the insects, spiders, rodents, and snakes that he regularly finds hiding beneath the litterfall. He talked about the hawks and owls that use the trees for roosts and for nests. He told me that certain squirrels had even developed a taste for the pungent eucalyptus berries. The more he talked, the more chagrined—and intrigued—I got.

The next time I walked in a eucalyptus forest, instead of speeding through it I slowed down. I looked around, turned over logs, listened keenly, and sat down in inconspicuous places to watch the goings on. I noticed how little birds were building nests under the furls of bark on the trees, and under one furl I once discovered a sleepy, confused bat. Among the tree tops I noticed the jays who were forever carrying on their family squabbles. I saw juncos and towhees picking over the ground, and in the spring I saw how the swarms of bees attracted to the eucalyptus flowers were themselves attracting the attention of shrikes and other insect-eating birds. I also noticed a squirrel tasting a eucalyptus berry, and I saw where mice had girdled a young eucalyptus sapling by eating the bark. At night I heard the cracklings and stirrings of hundreds of unseen animals. In truth I have found the eucalyptus forest to be a fairly rich and exciting place, as these strange Australian trees and the familiar California wildlife work out a relationship that is brand new in the history of the world.

Besides the eucalyptus forest, Kennedy Grove bears the signs of still another grand-scale commercial venture that didn't pan out. The California and Nevada Railroad, chartered in the 1880s, ran through the middle of the park. Its ambitious owners intended it to run from Emeryville to the mines of Utah and Nevada, but, alas, it never got past Orinda. The trip from Emeryville was apparently very pleasant, as the narrow-gauge train carried its load of farmers and sightseers through the San Pablo Creek Valley. But the return trip was somewhat embarrassing. Because there was no turntable at the end of the line, the train had to run backwards all the way from Orinda to the Bay.

Two picnic areas in Kennedy Grove are named after nearby stops on the railroad: Frenchman's Curve and Clancy's Place.

What does the future hold for Kennedy Grove? Many of the crowded eucalyptus trees have been thinned out as part of the design of the picnic area, and the ground is irrigated to keep the lawns green. I imagine that in another fifty or sixty years the thinning and the steady watering will result in some of the most magnificent and massive eucalyptus in the state.

Directions: From Oakland, take Highway 24 through the Caldecott tunnel to the Orinda turnoff. Exit here and go left (north) onto Camino Pablo which eventually changes into San Pablo Dam Rd. At the northern end of the San Pablo Reservoir (approximately 5 miles from the freeway) turn right onto Castro Ranch Rd. and then right again onto Hillside Dr. to the park.

Las Trampas

Las Trampas is over 3,000 acres of East Bay wilderness. Golden eagles are regularly sighted here, gliding smoothly and silently over the meadows, still regal even though there are no longer Indians in these valleys to collect their feathers and worship them as gods. Mountain lions prowl the rugged ridges, tending their herds of deer. Red foxes, gray foxes, bobcats, ringtails, raccoons, skunks, coyotes, and weasels—shy and secretive animals—hunt throughout the broad, benevolent valleys and steep side canyons. Yet despite the best efforts of these skillful hunters, squirrels, mice, and rabbits lead fat, bold, and prosperous lives.

Supporting this rich and varied wildlife are the rich and varied environments of Las Trampas. Northwest of Eagle's Peak, in the Corduroy Hills area, is a big, forested canyon, as nearly unexplored as any area in the East Bay. The woodlands are sprinkled with open meadows— meadows which in spring are like bowls spilling over with flowers and bird songs. The south-facing (sun-facing) slopes of Las Trampas Ridge support a spicy-smelling diminutive forest of chaparral bushes. Sycamores and bay trees shade the creeks, while most of the slope that leads up to Rocky Ridge is a vast, treeless meadow of grasses and spring wildflowers. And everywhere are huge slabs of rock, tossed and crumpled, fragmented and compacted, uplifted and worn down again by millions of years of geological indecision and revolt.

These many different environments create niches for many rare animals, birds, and plants. But rarest of all, the very richness of the park gets us to re-examine the so-called ordinary world around us. It was here, for example, that I discovered the wind. We usually take the wind for granted. But Rocky Ridge rises two thousand feet above sea level, and it has some of the most extraordinary wind that can be found in the Bay Area.

Wind does not just blow mechanically, like the current of dull, lifeless air produced by an electric fan. It has infinite variety. Most of the time it is light and whimsical. It slaps you playfully on the cheek, tickles you near the ear, tousles your hair. One gust is warm and languid, another cool, sharp, and clear. One minute it blows with the determination of a grand opera, and then it trails off forgetfully into nothing. Even the most savage, biting wind pauses now and then in its howling for a moment of lyrical refreshment. As you reach the ridgetop you might sit down somewhere, close your eyes, and give yourself over to the wind. It can leave you as refreshed as if you had just stepped out of the hands of a master masseur.

How does the landscape react to thousands of years of wind? Along Rocky Ridge you will find a large stone outcropping that is pockmarked with caves. These caves are thought by many to be sculptures of the wind. Look inside them for a view of miniature Bryce Canyons with their sandstone swirls, circular gouges, archways, tunnels, and cornucopias—the strangely soothing, whimsical calligraphy of the wind.

I've spent many days hiking through Las Trampas, and I've found it to be a remote, primitive experience with only two exceptions. One is the Little Hills Ranch area near the park entrance. Owned by the East Bay Regional Park District and operated by a concessionaire, Little Ranch offers group picnic sites with such civilized features as a swimming pool, playground, stocked fishing hole, game areas, horseback riding stables, and a dance area. For more information, call (415) 837-0821 or 837-7076.

Another exception to the wilderness character of Las Trampas is Rocky Ridge Road, a paved road that bisects the park and leads to a military communications installation beyond the park's boundaries. Yet in the springtime all sorts of unusual bugs (the unsung wildlife of Las Trampas) come tumbling out of the grasslands onto the pavement where they can be watched and appreciated by those hiking up the steep slope.

But Rocky Ridge Road is untypical of Las Trampas's trails. Most of them are delightfully narrow, unsophisticated footpaths that bring you close to the wildlife and lead you unobtrusively through the forests and meadows up to the ridgetops. They are trails where you can become intimate with your immediate surroundings while gazing out across vast panoramas.

Both of the ridgetops in this park (Las Trampas Ridge and Rocky Ridge) are prominent landmarks in the Bay Area, and each provides an utterly spectacular view. From Las Trampas Ridge you can look out over the San Ramon Valley, where Mount Diablo looms up close, like a huge mother hen brooding over her flock of little chick hills. From Rocky Ridge you can see the vast parallel ridges of the Coast Range extending toward the Bay and southward. I am always heartened by this view of so many square miles of still wild, undeveloped land remaining in the East Bay.

From these ridgetops there is, however, an even more distant, mind-expanding view. You can find it by looking, not out to the horizon, but down at your feet. Examine the rocks on the ridgetops, and you are likely to find the remains of clamshells embedded in them—sure evidence that these towering ridges were once underwater. In fact at various times this area was an ocean dotted with islands. Fossils found in and around Las Trampas also show that this area once consisted of plains and marshes where mastodons and camels grazed alongside other equally improbable animals. In still more distant times the charming meadows and forests you can see from the ridgetops were a stark landscape of hissing volcanoes.

The saga of geological change is one of the truly grand and heroic tales that modern science has given us. Forces within the earth have thrust up immense mountain chains, and these mountain chains have time and again been worn back to the sea. And the mighty forces that wear down mountains are all around, constantly and often visibly at work.

Aside from the wind with its delicate sculpturings, a second powerful force of erosion is water. One of the best water shows takes place in Devil's Hole, a box canyon west of Rocky Ridge. This is an area of massive stone outcroppings and rugged slopes. For several days after a rainstorm water seeps out through cracks on the stony ledges, flows in sheets down the rock faces, and gathers itself into a splashing, cascading little creek.

Stop at this creek some day and spend a half hour or so playing with the water, running it through your fingers, looking at its formlessness (it takes its shape "negatively," from whatever solids contain it), feeling its coolness, and watching all its delightful tricks. Water is so common that we take it for granted. But look at water freshly some time. Pretend that you are from outer space and have just arrived on earth. You find a clear pool in the creek. It looks hard and flat, like a big metallic jewel. You step into it and it shatters. Heartbroken, you withdraw your foot, but the jewel reforms itself as perfect as before. You bring out a magnifying glass, but you cannot find any sign of where the water was broken. The more you study the pool the stranger it gets. It reflects light, yet you can see through it. It's colorless, yet plainly visible. You try to pick some of this water up, but it slips through your fingers. The longer you play with it the more oddities you discover, until you are certain that you have just happened upon the most incredible substance in the whole universe—which may very well be true.

Another erosive force on these ridges is lichen. Lichen, which looks like splotches and crusts on the rocks, is a combination of two primitive plant forms—a fungus and an alga—that have become linked together as if they were a single plant. Lichen exudes a mild acid that imperceptibly but steadily breaks down the rocks, turning them into soil. The soil will, for a while, sustain plants, until eventually it is washed downhill by the water or blown away by the winds.

It is hard to believe, except in the most abstract and theoretical way, that lichen, wind, and water will eventually wear these ridges flat. But as humans we can observe this land for only a handful of hours. Lichen, wind, and water will be at work for millions of years. And they will never give up—not until, grain-by-grain, they finally grind these ridges down to sea level again. Pause along the trail sometime and get acquainted with lichen, wind, water, and embedded clamshells. They can open the door through which you can step from Las Trampas into another consciousness—the immense consciousness of geological time.

Directions: From Highway 680 south of Danville, take the Crow Canyon Rd. exit in San Ramon. Head west along Crow Canyon Rd. to Bollinger Canyon Rd. and turn right. The park entrance is at the end of Bollinger Canyon Rd., about 4.5 miles.
    See Map H.

Mission Peak

Mission Peak, at 2,517 feet above sea level, is a mere midget among world-class mountains. Yet it rises so abruptly out of the Fremont plains, thrust up a half-mile into the air, and it presents such a massive and monumental aspect to the tiny world below it, that from the moment I laid eyes on it I ignored the statistics and gave it the respect and admiration that I would accord any other great mountain. Even when speeding past it on a freeway, I could not help sending it a wistful sidelong glance that said, "You are a spectacular little mountain, and I will surely get to know you better some day."

Our acquaintance, nevertheless, was delayed for many years. And what finally led me to Mission Peak Regional Preserve, the 2,600-acre park that surrounds and includes the peak, was not its topographical prominence. Nor was it the urge to experience the panoramic view I could expect from its summit, or a simple desire to explore its great, grassy slopes and wooded valley. What ultimately drew me here were reports of its stone walls.

I have seen similar stone walls elsewhere in the East Bay—in Morgan Territory on the eastern slopes of Mount Diablo, on Round Top Peak in the Oakland Hills, and near Vollmer Peak in Tilden Regional Park. They are rather squat, no more than knee high, and they tend to follow ridgetops in high, remote areas. At some time in the past, great effort must have been expended to haul these large stones up the slope and put them in place. But no one knows who did it—or when, or why. These walls have no discernible practical value, they follow no known property lines, and there is no historical record to explain their existence. An unproven rumor has it that they are of great antiquity, some people claiming that they predate the Spanish, others even insisting that they predate the Indians who once lived here. But no one can tell for sure. They are a mystery. Whenever a local newspaper would do an article on one of them. I would often be approached for my opinion. For years, all I could do was shrug my shoulders and say lamely, "I don't know."

So it is that on a hot summer's day I decide to visit Mission Peak Preserve, to search out the stone walls, to sit among them for a few hours, to think about them deeply, and perhaps to understand something of their mystery. It is already past noon, and I choose the Stanford Avenue entrance to the preserve, which offers a direct, if steep, three-mile hike up a predominantly grassy slope to the summit.

As I start up the fire road, I meet an old man wearing a flannel shirt (despite the heat) and carrying a light day pack. We stop to talk. He retired several years before, he tells me, and now he spends all his time wandering through these hills.

"Do you know where I can find the stone walls?" I ask.

He smiles knowingly and spreads out his hand, showing me the back of it. The trail forks here, he explains, stretching out his fingers. And this is the peak, he goes on, pointing to his knuckle. If you walk along here. . .

I keep staring at his hand. It is an old man's hand, gnarled by age and arthritis. Purple veins, like mountain streams, crisscross its weathered skin. I look up into his face, and am startled by the youthful, playful eyes looking back at me. If I am searching for mysteries, I think to myself, this is certainly an auspicious beginning.

The hike toward the summit is long, and on this day, tiring. The grasses around me are dried, the sun hot, and the air still. My head bowed to the ground, I notice the soil at my feet. The earth is dry and hard-baked, as impenetrable, it seems, as concrete, with huge, deep cracks.

I push on toward the summit, still looking at the soil. About halfway to the top I come upon signs of a landslide from the previous winter. A chunk of land, perhaps eight or ten acres, seems to have pulled loose from the side of the mountain and moved several yards down the slope.

I stop at the landslide to rest. Despite my best efforts to concentrate on the mysterious walls, I find myself thinking about the soil beneath me. What would make soil harden and crack in the summer heat, move and slump in the winter rains? I review what I know of geology and find that this slope provides an almost textbook-perfect illustration of what I have read about the clay soils of the East Bay. Individual clay particles, when seen under a microscope, are made of thin plates. When it rains, these plates absorb water and expand like little accordions. When the water evaporates, the "folds" of the accordion collapse and the particles shrink in size.

Clay also has "cohesion"—the quality that makes it so valuable to potters. The water on both the inside and the outside of the clay particles interacts chemically with each particle—it is called "ionization"—so that the water, in effect, serves as a glue that binds the particles together. Thus instead of the individual particles expanding in the rain and rolling one-by-one down the hills, the entire mass of soil holds together, growing and swelling, until finally the weight is so great that a huge block of soil detaches itself from the underlying soils and moves with a massive slumpage down the hill. Similarly, as the soil dries in the summer heat, the "glue" still holds and the earth cracks at intervals, rather than just collapsing the way sand might.

After resting a while, I continue toward the summit, aware for the first time of a tentative movement in the air. I feel it first as a slight, gentle tickling of the cheek, a random arousal among the grasses. The thistles that line the trail's edge shudder ever so faintly now and then. As the afternoon progresses, these "thermal" breezes—caused by the air rising from the hot ground and cooler air sweeping in to take its place—become stronger and steadier. Wild oats on the meadow, whose dry husks were hanging limp and languid earlier in the day, now come alive, all trembling and straining hard, like tiny flags on thin, bent masts, all lined up in the breeze to point the way to the top of the mountain. They remind me of the row of flags at United Nations Plaza in New York, each tiny oat husk (it seems to me) representing a tiny and unique nation.

The winds through the grasses seem to trigger excitement among the grasshoppers. Straw-like, apparently as dry and withered as the oat husks, they now hop into the air and fall back to earth. As I detour from the trail and walk through the grass, hundreds of them explode all around me, like popcorn in a kettle.

The higher I climb on Mission Peak, the stronger the wind, the thinner the soil, the shorter the grasses. As I near the top, I come upon a bare, almost craggy area. Cattle congregate here in clumps, bringing to mind picture-postcard scenes of the Swiss Alps. Vultures, borne effortlessly by the strong thermal updrafts, circle higher and higher on motionless, outstretched wings. A sparrow hawk, with only an occasional twitch and flutter, remains frozen in the air. A glider, also playing in the thermal currents, looks so stiff compared with the advanced grace of the sparrow hawk and vultures, that this product of modern technology appears curiously primitive and pre-historic by comparison.

I study the hawk, vultures, and glider, and by watching them I find that I can "see" the air. I can "see" the thick places and the thin places, the strong places and the weak. The air, in motion and alive, now seems as palpable and "real" as the earth below. The earth, too, is alive and in motion, the signs of its swelling and shrinking being clear indications of a great, slow, seasonal breathing. And in the warmth of the day, I feel very much like a kid, "tucked in" and secure, between the living mattress of earth and the living blanket of air.

Is this, I wonder, how the Indians understood the world—the earth alive, the air alive, trees and even rocks alive, all independently alive yet bound together in a great web? This thought in mind, I pause for a while at the summit of Mission Peak, looking over the South Bay and the plains of Fremont, meditating on the changes that have taken place in the last two centuries. The once massive Alviso Marshes have been diked and turned into pastel-colored salt-evaporating ponds. On the flatlands below, a few dozen tule houses have been replaced by tens of thousands of tract homes. Pronghorn antelopes that used to run through the meadows below in herds of two and three hundred have been supplanted by lines of cars. Freeways and boulevards have superseded the foot trails that once radiated from Indian villages. The roar one hears is not that of a grizzly bear, but of a diesel truck gearing down.

But history does not just disappear. Below me are the shellmounds of Coyote Hills which mark the site of a large Ohlone village at the mouth of Alameda Creek. Closer to the foot of the mountain is Mission San Jose and, to the west of it, the Ohlone Indian cemetery.

And, of course, there are the stone walls.

I follow the old man's directions and find them easily. Crumbled and settled, they are no more than a foot or two high, and they extend along a ridge on the eastern slope. As I walk slowly along their length, I think about what people have said about them. I have heard over the years much wild speculation about how they were astronomical markers put here by ancient Chinese explorers. There have been dark rumors of an ancient, pre-Indian civilization with great cities and advanced technologies. I have even heard it suggested that they were guides for the spaceships of extraterrestrial visitors. I really don't know about any of this. I won't make a big point of it—I hate to be one to squelch the imagination—but I personally tend to dismiss these lines of speculation as the flamboyance and silliness of a world whose tastes are so jaded that only the utterly theatrical and garish can rouse the mind to interest.

What are my own ideas about these walls? I tried my best that afternoon, but in truth I still don't have any. It was hardly typical of the Indian people of this area to move rocks and build walls. It has been suggested that they might have been sheep pens, but they do not form enclosures the way sheep pens should. Since these high and dry hills were surely never farmed, I doubt if the rocks were moved to make the ground ready for plowing, as was the case in New England fields. They do not to follow tribal boundaries, nor the property lines of either the Spanish land grants or the Anglo ranches that followed them.

In truth, I do not know why these rocks were hauled up to the ridgetops and aligned this way. I do not know who put them here, or when. And, to be honest, I find that I enjoy not knowing. The past is indeed a strange country, and I love to explore it not only for the knowledge it reveals, but for the mysteries it holds. As I walk back along the trail, back down those outstretched fingers on the old man's hand, I feel a curious sense of victory. I came, I saw, but (what relief!) I did not conquer. The mystery of the stone walls is, I am delighted to report, still alive and well on Mission Peak.

Directions: From Highway 880 (the Nimitz Freeway), exit at Durham Rd. in Fremont. Follow Durham Rd. east to Mission Blvd., then turn left on Mission. The Ohlone College entrance to the park can be found by turning right onto the campus. Parking is available near the swimming pool.

The Stanford Ave. entrance can be reached by following Durham Rd. and turning right (south) on Mission Blvd., then left (east) onto Stanford Ave. The parking area is at the end of Stanford, past the Weibel Winery.

See Map I.

Morgan Territory

The county road that leads to Morgan Territory in the ridges east of Mount Diablo seems to have been built to keep people away from this 2,160-acre park. It is an extremely narrow, one-lane road that winds and twists up the slopes—the sort of mountain road that you might almost expect to find in Nepal and Bhutan. If two cars meet, one of them must pull over onto whatever approximation of a shoulder can be found, while the other edges past. This road obviously was not made to move hordes of commuters swiftly from their homes to their jobs; rather, it is a remnant of the one-lane roads that covered most of rural America in the age of horse travel. In fact, if there were to emerge around one of the steep curves a one-horse shay with a farmer in his Sunday best, jiggling the reins and urging his horse with soft words ("Gee-yup, Bessie, old girl. Gee-yup.") I would be delighted, to be sure, but hardly surprised.

Morgan Territory Regional Preserve feels to me like the most remote of all the East Bay Regional Parks. Away from the major air routes and far from the Bay Area population centers, it also tends to be one of the quietest. With most of the park more than 2,000 feet above sea level, it has an airy, top-of-the-world feeling to it. Well-graded fire roads loop easily and invitingly over its meadows and through its oak woodlands. Blue oaks and live oaks form open, pleasant groves with a sparse understory, mostly of manzanita. The trees that comprise these groves are young, healthy, and well-formed; but it is the occasional grandfather oaks, solitary giants of prodigious dimensions, growing alone in the meadows, that command one's attention. In generations past, these ancient ones grew among other trees; but gradually they overshadowed their companions, attaining first dominance, then—as their roots pulled in more and more of the scarce water—isolation. They now stand alone, their massive trunks in decay, most of their grand limbs sheared off, their foliage often reduced to the sparsest imaginable crown of delicate new leaves. Acorn woodpeckers have riddled them with holes; their trunks are splotched with lichen. Ancient and in grand ruin, they are strongly reminiscent of the great, crumbling medieval castles of Europe.

In contrast to these solitary and monumental oaks are the vivid wildflowers. Thousands upon thousands of purple sanicles, tidy tips, phacelias, lupines, clarkias, buttercups, and dozens of other varieties gather on these lofty meadows for their annual spring reunion as indeed they have gathered every year for tens of thousands of years.

So many rocks and boulders are scattered throughout the park that in places you feel that you are walking through an immense rock garden. These rocks, themselves gray and old, nurture many older life forms. There are lichens of many shapes and colors (sulphur yellow, apricot orange, rust, olive green, and chocolate brown) that cover their tops, mosses that grow on their shaded sides, and ferns that sprout from their bases—all ancient plants that prospered long before the arrival of the more highly-evolved flowering plants. The animal life includes lizards that dash out from the crevices to do push-ups in the sun, snakes that slither beneath the rocks for protection, and salamanders that live in the moist soil under the rocks—reptiles and amphibians that flourished in their present form long before the coming of the warm-blooded mammals.

I was once musing about this curious assemblage of antiquities, when something else in the rocks caught my eye: mortar holes from a bygone Indian people. These shallow, cuplike holes were not made by the Ohlones of the San Francisco Bay area, nor by the Miwoks of the San Ramon Valley and Delta. Rather, I believe, they were made by a Yokuts people who lived just to the east of

Morgan Territory, along the sluggish San Joaquin River and its maze of channels, sloughs, and great tule marshes.

One time I took my daughter, Sadie, then ten years old, on a hike into Morgan Territory. It was late November, the day after Thanksgiving in fact. The first rains had fallen recently, and I spent much of the morning on my hands and knees, studying the new sprouts and attempting to guess from these first odd-shaped leaves what kinds of grasses and flowers would be growing here the following spring. A daddy with his nose in the ground is no ten-year-old's idea of fun, and Sadie, always the spirit of adventure, suggested that we eat our lunch on top of the highest rock we could find in all Morgan Territory. We climbed a ridge, then climbed a rock, and unwrapped our sandwiches. The view was remarkable. To the north we could glimpse part of the Delta with its sloughs, tule-choked islands, and meandering rivers sparkling in the sun. Far to the east were the snow-capped peaks of the Sierra, looking strangely like whitecaps on a distant sea. Beneath us, stretched out for miles and miles, as flat it seemed as an ocean, was the Central Valley.

The Central Valley, I realized then, was for both of us virtually *terra incognita*—a place we passed through many times on the way to the Sierra, but never stopped to explore. But here, at what felt like the top of the world, I recalled the words that Lieutenant José María Estudillo, commander of the Presidio of Monterey, wrote in his diary when looking over this valley in 1819. "The view from south to north is beautiful," he wrote, "for its end cannot be seen, with its lakes, swamps, and groves of trees."

Dams, diversions, and other flood control works keep the San Joaquin River from spreading out onto the valley floor, as it did then. But from where we are sitting this broad valley, as haze-filled as in a dream, evokes an image of what once existed. We can easily imagine the great flocks of migrating ducks and geese that would have moved into the valley at this time of year, skeins of them threading the air, clouds of them rising up from patches of still water and then settling back down. The fall run of king salmon would have been well underway, and perhaps from our rock we might have been able to see Yokuts men in tule rafts, spreading their salmon nets against the flow of the water. Smoke might be rising from villages located on hillocks throughout the marshlands, and perhaps we might catch sight of the women repairing the tule-mat walls of their homes in preparation for the winter rains. If the wind was blowing from the east, we might even hear the "chuck-chuck-chuck" of their pestles as they ground acorns for the evening meal—acorns that had probably been collected from the very same oaks we had been admiring earlier in the day.

The name "Morgan Territory" suggests a frontier. For the Yokuts people of the Central Valley, this would indeed have been a frontier—the westernmost boundary of their watery world, the rim of the basket in which they had lived for hundreds of years. For Sadie and me, too, this was a frontier. We are a "Bay Area" people, and these easternmost slopes of the Mount Diablo Range are at the very edge of our territory. It is a strange, foreign country that we view below, populated by different animals, different plants, different people. "The view from south to north is beautiful," I can hear Estudillo saying, and although greatly changed since the time he first saw it, from where we are sitting it still is beautiful.

"Someday we'll have to get to know the land down there better," I tell Sadie. But she has already finished her lunch, scrambled down from our perch, and is racing across the meadow. After leaving a few scraps of bread for the birds, I shove the remains of our lunch into the backpack and run to catch up with her.

"Where do you think the Indian houses were?" she asks when, on our way back, we pause to rest at the mortar holes.

I examine the site more critically, and realize that there were probably never houses here at all. This was not a village, I speculate, but at best a temporary encampment. Perhaps, I explain, Yokuts men on a hunting expedition would spend the night here. Perhaps families collecting seeds in the spring or acorns in the fall would camp here for a few days. And, given the borderland quality of the place, it is very likely that the Yokuts and the Bolbones, a Bay Miwok people from the western slopes of Mount Diablo, might have arranged to meet here for their annual trading.

We fall silent, and in these remote and lofty meadow-lands we can almost picture them. We imagine a line of Yokuts straggling up the slopes from the east. They are dressed in deer skins and tule skirts, the heavy burden baskets slung over their backs filled with trade goods: obsidian and bow-making wood from the Sierra, unusual foods from the Valley. From the west we can picture a line of Bolbones, their baskets and carrying nets filled with abalone shells from the Pacific Ocean and red cinnebar ore from the Santa Clara Valley. How tired these people must be from having walked all day with heavy baskets up these mountains. How excited they must be with the anticipa-tion of meeting each other, hearing a strange language, and acquiring exotic goods. And how utterly astounded they will be when they find a bald, bearded man and his ten-year-old daughter standing by the mortar holes, patiently awaiting their arrival.

Directions: From Highway 580 at Livermore, exit at the North Livermore Ave. turnoff and head north (away from town). At the end of North Livermore Ave., turn left onto Manning Rd., then right (north) onto Morgan Territory Rd. which leads to the park entrance.

To reach Morgan Territory from the Concord area, take Highway 680 north to the Ygnacio Valley Rd. exit in Walnut Creek. Follow Ygnacio Vally Rd. east to Clayton Rd. and turn right. Pass through the town of Clayton onto Marsh Creek Rd., then turn right (south) onto Morgan Territory Rd.

See Map J.

Ohlone

There is no easy way of getting to Ohlone Regional Wilderness, a huge park of nearly seven thousand acres in the high ridges of southern Alameda County. Most of the park is three thousand feet or more above sea level, and it is far from any public road. It can be reached from Sunol Regional Wilderness on the west or from Del Valle Regional Recreation Area on the north, but from either direction you have a long uphill hike just to get to its boundaries. This is not a park for those in a hurry; you can't just drop in for an hour or two. A visit to Ohlone Wilderness demands a full day's commitment, maybe more.

Because Ohlone Wilderness is so remote and relatively inaccessible, you encounter few of the family groups you find in other regional parks. The only people you generally meet here are hardy backpackers. Sometimes after hiking alone for hours you are surprised to hear the thud of vibram boots on the trail ahead and the clinking of cookware. When a pair of hikers comes into view, you notice their towering backpacks outfitted with sleeping bags, tents, and tightly-rolled foam pads. Hours may pass before you see another backpacker. These are the kind of outdoors people you would expect to meet in the high Sierra, and they have been coming to Ohlone Wilderness ever since the land was opened to back-country camping in the spring of 1987.

But Ohlone Wilderness is not, of course, the high Sierra. This is Coast Range wilderness. The trail system consists mostly of old ranching roads that wind up and over the rounded shoulders of the ridges. You occasionally walk through open meadowland, and at times descend into valleys with year-round creeks, shaded by dense forests of big-leaf maples, sycamores, bays, alders, and willows.

But most of the land is open oak woodland—vast meadows dotted with blue oaks, valley oaks, and live oaks. Widely spaced, the trees reach immense proportions and full development. Each tree stands isolated, a kingdom unto itself—fully matured, its long history written deeply into the furrows of its bark, an utterly individualistic and magnificent creation.

"A very pleasant and enchanting lawn situated amid a grove of trees," is how George Vancouver, who visited the Bay Area in 1789, described a typical Bay Area oak woodland, comparing it not to a deep forest but to an English park. At Ohlone Wilderness you cannot help but stray from the official trail—the land is so open and inviting that it simply draws you in. In springtime you tread ankle-deep in carpets of wildflowers. Even in early summer mariposa lilies and harvest brodiaeas glow softly around your feet. You are not alone in these groves of great trees. Ground squirrels stand tautly at attention as you approach, then—when you get too close—dash headlong into their holes. Scrub jays, magpies, acorn woodpeckers, and flickers fly from tree to tree, their lines of flight easy and loping, like hammocks strung between the trees in the lazy heat of summer.

It takes a long time to reach the high oak woodland of Ohlone Wilderness, and I generally arrive there in late morning or early afternoon. The winds have died down by then. The trees are as motionless as stone, and unless there is a flock of jays present the oak woodland is a palace of silence. I wander to my heart's content, looking up into the trees, admiring the great sweep of the branches, rejoicing in the pregnant stubbiness of the twigs, marveling at the miraculous tension of the leaves as they hold themselves stiffly yet delicately out toward the sun. By late afternoon a gentle breeze often arises, and the leaves on the trees flutter slightly, rubbing against one another to produce a hushed whisper. As the breezes increase, the branches rock slightly, adding an almost inaudible creaking sound to the whisperings of the leaves. Each tree seems to be chanting its own hymn, and the mixing of their voices reminds me of a choir of Gregorian monks, solemnly swaying and praising the glories of earth and heaven.

I choose a place to camp—there are three such areas set aside for overnight camping in Ohlone Wilderness—eat a token supper, and as dusk approaches lay my sleeping bag under the oaks. I lie awake watching how the color drains slowly out of the trees, until by night they become gnarled silhouettes. Owls, in outline looking strangely like cats, come to roost in the branches. The night whisperings of the trees are different in tone from those of the day, and I fall asleep while listening to their vespers. At dawn I awake early and watch the pale light as it first touches the tops of the trees, then pours with breath-taking speed down their branches and trunks, and finally spills onto the earth. Full color returns to the trees; day has arrived, and I am eager to continue my wanderings.

My favorite destination in Ohlone Wilderness is Rose Peak. It is ten miles from either the Sunol or Del Valle entrance, and while it can be reached on a long day's hike, anyone packing too much weight—either in a backpack or around the waist—will find it formidable. Once there, though, Rose Peak offers a vista of seemingly limitless wild land all around it. Ridges and valleys reach out for miles, beyond which are splendid views of the Santa Clara Valley, the San Francisco Bay, and the Santa Cruz Mountains. At the summit you feel that you have reached close to the top of the world, apparently at eye level with Mount Diablo, Mount Tamalpais, and Mount Hamilton. Indeed, with an altitude of 3,817 feet, Rose Peak is only thirty-two feet lower than Mount Diablo. Yet unlike these other mountains, few people have ever heard of it, in part because it is so remote and because no paved road leads to the top, but more because instead of rising up out of a flatland with the drama of the other mountains, it is only a slight protuberance on an extensive plateau of land over three thousand feet high. I remember once arriving at the summit, justly proud of my great accomplishment, when my feat was put into proper perspective by the sight of a diminutive warbler who had (I suspect) just arrived from Central America with absolutely no fanfare.

On my long hikes through Ohlone Wilderness—there are no other—I often reflect on what the Ohlone Indians would have thought about the "wilderness" designation. After several thousand years of living in the Bay Area, this land was, of course, no more a wilderness to them than any of the rest of the East Bay. Although their permanent villages were along the bayshore and in the valleys, this land was certainly well visited and well used. Groups of men would have climbed into these ridges and spread themselves out, hiding behind rocks and trees, as they prepared for the pronghorn antelope drives. Hunters, with antler headdresses, regularly stalked the woodlands for deer. Family groups camped seasonally in ancestral plots to gather roots, seeds, and acorns. In summer, as was their custom, they burned the land to foster seed-bearing annual plants and make the meadows more hospitable for game. Every inch of the land was well explored and frequently visited. Individual rocks had names and stories attached to them. A rock, for example—which to our eyes would be nondescript and scarcely noticed—was a person once, and everyone knew the story of how that person was transformed. Particular crags were known for special powers, and boys undergoing initiation were sent to sleep on these crags to receive sacred dreams. The land was rich in stories and mythic qualities. There were hundreds, probably thousands, of places that were named and known—a far cry from today when a map of the area is almost entirely devoid of place names and cultural associations. The truth is that in Indian times these lands were used far more intensely and known far better than they are today. To us this land might be "wilderness"; to the Indians it was home.

With the passing of Ohlone tribal ways, we have lost several thousand years of accumulated cultural knowledge, and the pleasures that Ohlone Wilderness offers us are necessarily of a different kind. But they are extraordinary pleasures nonetheless. On two separate occasions, for example, when hiking out of Ohlone Wilderness toward Del Valle, I sighted a bald eagle. A glimpse of it in the distance—even before it got close enough for me to see its white head and white tail band—stopped me in my tracks. With only two or three easy, fluid, authoritative strokes of its wings it moved effortlessly an immense distance through the canyon toward me. A red-tailed hawk, which until then I thought represented the pinnacle of powerful flight, seemed by comparison to be fluttering and ineffectual. A bald eagle is pure power. It has to be seen to be believed, and once you have observed one—even for a few moments—you instantly understand why this bird was worshipped as a god by the Indians. Indeed, for the Ohlones the eagle was not just any god, but was the World Creator himself.

The Indians are mostly gone, but in recent years their World Creator has returned, and (who knows?) perhaps he will again usher in an age when people call untamed land such as this their home.

Directions: Ohlone Wilderness may be approached through Del Valle Regional Park (see page 161) or Sunol Regional Park (see page 72).
   See Map K.

Redwood

Look at a map and you'll see that Redwood Park is shaped a lot like a mushroom—a magical mushroom of grassland, brush, and peaceful redwood forests.

   I worked at this 1,800-acre park for nearly three years in the early 1970s and I only dimly remember the initial impact the quiet, somber redwood forest made on me. "Are you *sure* this is Oakland?" I kept asking the fellow I was working with. But after several hundred (perhaps thousand) miles of hiking through Redwood Park I learned that Oakland is not just East 14th Street or the downtown Convention Center. It's also a place where you can find clumps of mushrooms, marmalade orange and sulphur yellow, glowing softly in the leaf litter of a dark forest. Where one night I counted twenty-three deer browsing on a single meadow, and where there are innumerable foxes, racoons, skunks, possums, owls, and hawks. Where clumps of Douglas irises bloom, often in the most unlikely places. Where on hot summer days vultures circle high above the meadows, scribing lazy helixes toward the sun. But most of all it is where there stands a vast forest of redwoods, lofty trees five to six feet in diameter and over a hundred feet tall. Very few hikers seem to know about this forest, and those who do are small, insignificant figures as they walk under the towering canopy, among the straight columns of the trunks, and through the gentle, nourishing gloom of the redwood forest.

   The forest looks ancient and permanent. Yet in fact the redwoods at Redwood Park are all youngsters, less than a century old. They are a race of adolescent giants rising out of the logged-off remains of what many botanists think was the most magnificent grove of redwoods the world has ever seen.

As far as I know there are no written records of what the original forest was like. Apparently grizzly bears and condors were fairly common. The trees were so immense that some of them were clearly visible from the Golden Gate sixteen miles away. In the days before lighthouses and buoys, ships entering the Bay used to line up with these landmark trees to avoid certain shoals.

But by the early 1850s the redwood forest was logged clean. The wood went into building Benicia, Martinez, Oakland, and San Francisco. The redwood forest became "a sea of stumps." But even the stumps were extraordinary. John Muir, Asa Gray, and Joshua Whitney (after whom Mount Whitney was named) were among the notables of that time who visited these "melancholy ruins" to marvel at the remains. Many of the stumps measured more than twenty feet across. One stump near the summit of Redwood Peak measured thirty-three feet in diameter, and may have been the largest redwood ever known. By comparison the largest (in diameter) redwood alive today is the Stout Tree in Jedediah Smith State Park, a mere twenty feet.

In the following decades, however, even the stumps were not to be spared. Woodchoppers swarmed over the hills, hacking down the stumps and grubbing out the roots for firewood. During the 1870s and 1880s the stumps supplied over half the firewood in the East Bay. And the trees which did resprout were cut down once more after 1906 to help rebuild San Francisco after the earthquake.

After the logging came a pastoral interlude in the history of Redwood Park, as settlers arrived with their cattle and their small farms. The stone building on Redwood Road, just east of the park entrance, was once the schoolhouse of these early settlers. Old Church Picnic Area was the site of their church. And even today you can find throughout the park the remains of their orchards—pear trees, apple trees, and plum trees that flower brilliantly each spring and still bear delicious fruit. The settlers were gradually moved out in the 1920s when the Water Company took over the land

as watershed. In the mid 1930s the Water Company passed the land on to the newly-formed East Bay Regional Park District.

In the late 1930s WPA crews arrived on the scene and built many of the park's roads and trails and erected the four stone huts that are scattered along Stream Trail. During the Second World War the park was used freely by various military units. Naval Air Cadets "lived off the land"—eating berries and trapping small game as part of their survival training. A camouflage unit, complete with cannons, tanks, bazookas, and half-tracks, played eerie games of hide-and-seek in the redwood forests. Strangest of all were the burial crews of 1,500 men who would set up a two-acre simulated cemetery complete with fencing, a signed entrance, and five hundred white crosses. Every two weeks a bulldozer would blade the area clean, and a new crew would arrive to repeat the macabre process.

Finally, the Park District itself has made minor efforts to "develop" parts of Redwood Park. Redwood Canyon is now a popular picnic area. Barricades, jumps, and an exhibition ring have been erected on Hunt Field for the equestrian set. And Roberts Recreation Area maintains a noisy, happy, high-energy mood throughout the summer with its heated outdoor swimming pool, children's playground and wading pool, and its redwood-shaded picnic tables.

This, then, has been the strange history of Redwood Park. But fortunately the latest chapter is being written once more by the trees. Despite the logging, the stump cutting, the root grubbing, the relogging, the settling, the grazing, and the exploits of the military, despite all that has happened to the land, the redwood trees have grown back once more. No wonder they are called *sempervirens*— always living.

Today the trees are less than a century old, but they have already regained their air of dignity and permanence. With their great size and a botanic history that stretches back 100 million years to the Age of Reptiles, the redwoods at

Redwood Park seem aloof from the modern world. The leaf litter and thick duff have carpeted the forest floor, and it takes a practiced eye to find signs of the previous logging. Now and then hikers find old ox-shoes or bits of metal from axes and saws. Flat areas (such as Millsite) mark the location of old sawmills. And hikers throughout the park, especially along Stream Trail, may spot old "skid roads," grooves gouged into the hillside that were originally greased with animal fat and along which the enormous logs were dragged.

Another sign of the logging is the way the trees grow. Throughout the forest most of the trees are arranged in circles. In the center of each circle is the ghost of a tree that grew a hundred years ago. Once the tree was felled, sprouting took place around the edges of the stump. The great size of some of these "family circles," as they are called, hints at how enormous the original trees once were—and suggests the great future in store for this land if we can manage to leave things alone for the next few thousand years.

In addition to its massive redwood forest, Redwood Park also has many hundreds of acres of grassland, brush, and (besides the redwoods) no fewer than three distinct forest environments. These other areas are so extensive that it's possible to hike for hours in Redwood Park without ever setting foot in a redwood grove. Near the northern corner of the park, above Girl's Camp, is a eucalyptus forest. Around Orchard Trail is a huge oak-bay-madrone forest—dense, often to the point of being impenetrable, and especially rich in wildlife. And a forest of Monterey pines can be found near the junction of West Ridge and French Trails. These pines were planted decades ago, perhaps to replace the logged-off redwoods. Misplaced natives of the Monterey Peninsula, they are now old and decayed, leaning precariously, their tops broken off by the winds. There is a gothic air about them, an air of defeated nobility, that makes this one of the most haunting areas of Redwood Park.

And finally there are the creeks that bounce and bubble in the spring, the grassland that forms intimate sunlit clearings in the forests and in the brush, and the remains of old orchards that reward observant hikers with an occasional handful of plums or apples.

There's grandeur and variety in these hills, only a bus ride away from downtown Oakland, making Redwood Park one of the best hiking parks in the East Bay. Judging from the moss-covered initials and dates carved into the rocks of Redwood Peak, hiking has been popular since the turn of the century. And considering the way the redwoods have been thriving, it will undoubtedly be even more popular in the centuries to come.

Directions: Take Highway 13 (the Warren Freeway) to the Redwood Rd. exit, and follow Redwood Rd. east, up the hill, beyond Skyline Blvd. The main entrance to Redwood Park can be reached by following Redwood Rd. east another 2 miles. Other entrances can be reached by turning left on Skyline Blvd. and following it along the crest of the Oakland Hills.

See Map L.

Sibley

Round Top Peak, which dominates the 386-acre Sibley Volcanic Regional Preserve, is a small, stoop-shouldered mountain in the Oakland Hills. It is only 1,761 feet high, and you would certainly never guess that it was once the most prominent volcano in the East Bay.

About ten million years ago a freshwater lake extended from what is now Tilden Park to the site of the San Leandro Reservoir. The volcano was born under the waters of this lake. When the lava stopped flowing, sediments from the lake settled over the lava deposits. Then volcanic activity began again. Geologists have counted eleven separate lava flows and at least two violent explosions in the birth of Round Top. The alternating volcanic and sedimentary layers were then folded, tilted, crumpled, and tossed by millions of years of earthquake activity.

The result has been geological complexity of the first magnitude, and Round Top has always been a favorite stomping ground for geologists. Aiding them in their research have been the quarries to the north of the peak, where years of commercial gouging have exposed old lava flows, mud flows, fault lines, vents, cinder piles, and other geologic forms. In 1977 the East Bay Regional Park District purchased some of these abandoned quarry sites, and created a self-guiding trail. A descriptive pamphlet is available at the park entrance.

After its traumatic geological history, you might imagine that Round Top would have settled down into the shabby retirement you would expect from a worn-out volcano. Far from it! In this century alone, Round Top has been changing identities with the startling rapidity of a model at a fashion show.

The park that surrounds Round Top Peak has been officially named Sibley Volcanic Regional Preserve after Robert Sibley, one of the founders of the East Bay Regional Park District. But the man who probably affected it most was Frank Havens, a turn-of-the-century millionaire and founder of the Mahogany Eucalyptus and Land Company. The purpose of this grandiose, ill-conceived company was to cover the crests of the Oakland-Berkeley Hills with great forests of eucalyptus trees. As Havens declared in a prospectus to potential stockholders, eucalyptus was "the most valuable tree on the face of the globe. No teak, mahogany, ebony, hickory, or oak was ever tougher, denser, stronger or of more glorious hardness." Not only did Havens promise riches, but he promised them fast, claiming that a eucalyptus sapling might grow five or six inches in a single day!

Between 1910 and 1913 Havens lured thousands of investors. He set up nine nurseries and an arboretum, and he employed as many as two hundred men at one time. Eucalyptus by the million were planted along the fourteen-mile stretch from North Berkeley to what is now Redwood Park. Round Top was at the center of Havens' empire, and it was Havens who had Skyline Boulevard built as a scenic drive to connect his various real estate and lumber holdings in the Oakland Hills. To give Havens credit, he undoubtedly believed in the infallibility of his eucalyptus empire. In 1913 he invited a forester to test-mill a few eucalyptus. And then he learned the terrible truth: the blue gum eucalyptus he had planted were worthless. It turned out that blue gum was never used for lumber in Australia, and the species of eucalyptus that the Australians did use were so slow growing that the trees could not be harvested until they were several hundred years old.

I don't know the name of the forester Havens hired, but someone ought to erect a monument in his honor. If he had found that eucalyptus was even half as valuable as Havens claimed, today the East Bay Hills would be the scene of one of a massive logging operation. The failure of blue gum is one of the luckiest things that has ever happened to the East Bay.

After the bubble burst, the eucalyptus forests were left alone. They were never thinned or in any way tended, and throughout most of this century Round Top's eucalyptus forest was virtually impenetrable. The trees stood tall and stringy. The undergrowth was a jungle of brush and litterfall. Leaves shimmered idly in the sun. On hot summer days it seemed as if the troubled wind had searched out the eucalyptus grove as a place to rest and sleep. At dusk a sudden stirring of the leaves and a creaking of the trunks announced that the winds were arousing themselves again, gathering themselves together like a caravan that would soon depart and leave the night-time forest strangely silent. These eucalyptus forests seemed as unchangeable as the hills themselves.

But in the winter of 1972–73 subfreezing weather struck the Bay Area and injured the eucalyptus trees. Round Top, with its relatively high, exposed location, was severely affected. The leaves died back and most of the trees seemed dead. Experts warned that these vast forests of dead and injured trees presented an extraordinary fire hazard, and newspapers spread images of fires roaring down the hills to consume the cities along the Bay.

In the spring of 1973 it was decided that the eucalyptus forests would have to go. That summer we heard the whining of chain saws and the crash of tall trees, and saw fleets of logging trucks roaring down the mountain roads with huge logs headed for the pulp mills. Big-time logging had finally arrived in the Oakland Hills. Frank Havens would have been delighted.

For several years Round Top was nearly denuded of eucalyptus. Bay trees, toyons, Monterey pines, coyote brush, poison oak, and coffee berry that had been suppressed in the shade of the eucalyptus now grew tall and vigorous. Grasses grew thick, and thousands of meadow wildflowers celebrated the disappearance of the eucalyptus with unconcealed exuberance. For a few years an unstable

environment was created, one that never existed before—
a California eucalyptus forest minus the eucalyptus.

There was much speculation about what would happen
to this environment. Would the grasses take over the hillside once again? Would the brush seize control of Round
Top as it had in large areas of nearby Tilden and Redwood?
Would the bay trees and toyons grow strong enough to
form the core of a mixed hardwood forest? Would the
Monterey pines consolidate themselves into a dark pine
forest? Or would the eucalyptus re-establish itself by
sprouting from roots and stumps?

Anyone acquainted with the complicated history of
Round Top might have predicted what is currently occur-
ring here: everything is happening at once! The grasslands,
brush, hardwoods, and Monterey pines all seem to be
flourishing beneath tall, young eucalyptus saplings that
have indeed resprouted. The vegetation, like the geology,
is now wonderously jumbled and confused. What kind of
wildlife will such an area attract? Which of the plant communities will eventually dominate? For the next few decades, Round Top will be attracting the attention of plant-
watchers and animal-watchers, in addition to the rock-
watchers who have always revelled in its complexity.

*Directions: Take Highway 24 through the Caldecott Tunnel to
Fish Ranch Rd. exit. Follow Fish Ranch Rd. to Grizzly Peak
Blvd. and turn left. Turn left again onto Skyline Blvd. The park
entrance can be found on the left, a short distance from the
intersection of Skyline Blvd. and Grizzly Peak Blvd.*

*Alternately, take the Joaquin Miller Rd. exit from Highway
13 (the Warren Freeway), and follow it east. Near the crest, turn
left onto Skyline Blvd. The entrance to Sibley is five miles from
this intersection along Skyline Blvd.*

Sunol

Many years ago, in the days when the Sunday drive was a major form of recreation, there existed a genteel ritual known as the "family picnic." Dad, mom, the kids, and some extra relatives (there were always extra relatives back then) would pack into the family buggy and sputter away to a park like Sunol. Here they spread their blankets along the shores of Alameda Creek. Like Spanish *conquistadors* they laid claim to the picnic tables and barbecue pits scattered along its banks. Small checkdams across the creek provided them with splash pools for swimming. Sunday artists set up their easels, kids swam and played ball, and grandfathers (dressed in Sunday suits and neckties) took off their shoes and let their liberated toes wiggle joyously in the cool grass. Here and there a stammering accordion could be heard. ("How well he plays, and he's only eleven!") The air smelled of hot dogs, pickles, and homemade pies. From the nearby woods, jays, squirrels, and mice could scarcely contain their excitement as they watched the potato chips rain upon the ground like manna.

Today this genteel ritual is still being practiced at Sunol Regional Wilderness—complete with splash pools, picnic tables, barbecue pits, and big noisy families. Sunol is also a favorite with still another group: hikers who park their cars near the entrance and with a backpack, an appropriate field guide, a map, binoculars, and a package of dried apricots head quickly away from the picnic areas. They follow miles of trails out into the wilds of Sunol, over the meadows, through the oak forests, up the mountains, and beyond to the distant ridges. They stop at the broad, rushing creek that gave Alameda County its name. They hike out into an enormously spacious land where there are still eagles, falcons, mountain lions, bobcats, and coyotes—out onto this big-hill, cow-dotted, almost Alpine wilderness.

The back-country of Sunol is mostly mountainous meadowland with open, sun-dappled forests of oak. Look closely at an oak some time, and you'll be amazed at how much unusual life it supports. Oak moth caterpillars build cobweb cities that cover the branches of some oak trees. There are lichens, mosses, and strange bugs in the furrows of the bark. One kind of lichen droops like Spanish moss from the branches. Birds build nests, while galls and mistletoes live out their curious existences.

Galls (or "oak apples") hang in bunches from the trees. A gall is formed when a wasp stings the bark of the tree and lays its eggs. The oak reacts by manufacturing a thick coating around the eggs to isolate them, and this thick coating is what we call the gall. It protects the oak tree against the hatching wasps, but at the same time it also protects the hatching wasps against their enemies. Within the closed gall the eggs produce small, white, bean-like larvae. The larvae eat their way through the tissues of the gall until they approach the outer shell where they pause and spin a cocoon. Here young wasps are born, tunnel the rest of the way through the gall, and fly out into the wide mysterious world to repeat the mating and egg-laying process. Other insects now crawl into the empty gall looking for leftover food. And woodpeckers drill into the old galls looking for other insects.

As for mistletoes, these grow in big clumps near the tops of the trees. They look like the nests of some gigantic bird when seen from the distance. They bear a crop of white berries that are poisonous to people. But birds eat the berries enthusiastically. Within each berry is a sticky, indigestible seed which the birds often rub off their beaks onto the surface of the tree. Here the seed germinates. The roots probe deep into the host tree, fastening themselves onto the life system of the oak and stealing food and moisture directly from the tree's tissues. Mistletoe is not, however, a complete parasite. It does have chlorophyll, and it manufactures some of its own food.

To the druids of Britain the mistletoe was the "golden

bough," the most sacred of all sacred plants. On the sixth night of the new moon a priest in white robes would climb the tree and cut down the mistletoe with a solid gold sickle. The plant was used for religious and medical rites. It was so valuable that the priests would sacrifice two white bulls to the gods in exchange for it. Of all the powerful rituals surrounding this plant, only a hint remains today: the quaint Christmas custom of kissing under the mistletoe.

To me the oak groves of Sunol with their light, airy mood and the strange life they support have a spiritual quality that is hard to describe. Spend some time here underneath the oak trees. After all, Buddha found enlightenment under a banyan tree. Sir Isaac Newton discovered gravity under an apple tree. Who knows which of the countless mysteries that still remain undiscovered will someday be revealed to someone sitting quietly underneath an oak tree in the East Bay hills?

Beyond the oak groves stretch the high meadowlands of Sunol. For an unusual and memorable experience try exploring these meadows by crossing them slowly, deliberately, and (please take me seriously) on all fours. Push your face into the grass and look really hard, until you find yourself totally immersed in the hidden world of sprouts, mouse tunnels, earth worm castings, gopher holes, and the epic journeys of bugs. You soon discover that all blades of grass are not alike. They may be thick or needle-thin, stiff or pliant, tall or short, whole or nibbled, smooth or fuzzy, and they come in a dozen different shades. If you focus all your attention on the ground, a clump of moss expands to the size of an Amazon rain jungle. Insects appear monstrous, fascinating, other-worldly. Scores of tiny, insignificant flowers you never noticed before now burn before your eyes like furnaces roaring away on the meadow floor. A small patch of meadowland can become incredibly vast.

If, while concentrating hard on the grass beneath you, a spring shower catches you in the middle of a field, consider yourself especially lucky. Get down on your belly so you won't miss a thing. A drop of rain falls, hits a blade of grass, and knocks it down. The raindrop then slides slowly off, and the grass, relieved of the weight, springs up again. As more drops fall, more blades of grass pop up and down until the whole field comes alive, wildly dancing in the rain, and creating one of the merriest sights you've ever seen.

The intimacy to be gained with the meadows and oak groves is one of the major joys of Sunol. But there are times when this intimacy is overshadowed by the immensity of the park and the land around it. From the top of McGuire Peak, Eagle's View, Vista Grande, Flag Hill, and other places within the park you can look out over distant storm-tossed mountains and valleys. Sunol Regional Wilderness itself is nearly 7,000 acres; and all around it are huge expanses of wild land that belong to the East Bay Regional Park District, the San Francisco Water Company, or to private ranchers. Trails (accessible by a permit available at the park entrance) connect Sunol with Mission Peak Regional Preserve to the west, and Ohlone Wilderness and Del Valle Regional Park to the east.

Needless to say, such an extensive wild area in Alameda County is in constant jeopardy. I was once hiking in Sunol when a jet plane whined overhead. Almost immediately, a

catbird hopped out of the brush to the top of a nearby tree and began to scold loudly at the plane, obviously protecting its territory. I understood the feeling. Those who love Sunol and the land around it have spent many years defending it against proposed guest ranches, subdivisions, and quarries. There have been stunning victories and a few distressing defeats.

Yet the fight to preserve this area is one of the most important in the Bay Area. It is this deep reservoir of uninterrupted wild land that makes possible the continued existence of eagles and mountain lions in the East Bay. If we can manage to keep the private ranch lands out of the hands of developers, and if we can prevent public lands from being futher degraded despite what will surely be great pressures in the future, then we can preserve, here in the East Bay, a wilderness area that approaches in scale and quality some of the State and Federal wilderness areas. We can preserve what is, in effect, the last extensive wilderness remaining in this part of the Diablo Range.

Directions: From Highway 680, exit at Calaveras Rd. in Sunol. Turn left (south) onto Calaveras Rd. to Geary Rd. The park entrance is at the end of Geary Rd.

For more information, a schedule of naturalist programs, or to reserve a campsite, call 862-2244.

See Map M.

Tassajara Creek

The name, "Tassajara," has such a lovely sound to it. You whisper it—*tah sah há rah*—and savor the images of beauty that come to mind. Then you wander into the library to find out what it means, and from the pages of a dry reference work the prosaic truth emerges. It comes from the Spanish signifying a place where beef is cut into strips and hung to dry—a place, in other words, where people once made beef jerky.

The park, like its name, is perhaps disappointing, not at all what you might expect from a regional park. There are no recreational facilities at Tassajara—no swimming pool, playground, or even picnic tables. There are no scenic crags, great views, or remote mountain terrain. There is not even, as far as I know, any rare or endangered plant or animal being protected here. Nor is there grandeur of scale; you can scarcely walk for a half hour in any direction without coming to a boundary fence.

Tassajara Creek Regional Open Space covers only about 450 acres of low-lying grassy hills. In most regards it is a very ordinary piece of land. And therein lies its rarity. The San Ramon and Livermore Valley area is one of the fastest growing regions in the state. Such ordinary land, now mostly cattle ranches, is fast getting gobbled up by subdivisions and industrial "parks." In the not too distant future, "ordinary" land in this area may be little more than a memory.

You can reach this park by taking Tassajara Road north from the Pleasanton area. From the parking lot the trail crosses Tassajara Creek. Although the entire park is named after this creek, in truth (yet another disappointment!) the creek just barely cuts across the southeastern corner of the park and is a very minor part of its landscape and mood. Once you emerge from the shade of the valley oaks, buckeyes, and willows that grow along its banks, you enter into a world of hummocky meadows that constitute almost all of this open space. (The only other trees here are some wonderfully large, gnarled willows that grow along a gully on the western edge of the park.) An asphalt road goes through the park to the top of a hill and a small, fenced-in military installation—a collection of stark white saucers and towers that give the impression of belonging somewhere in outer space. Except for the asphalt road, there are no trails to lead you over the land, and you can wander at will along the contours of these softly rounded, grass-covered hills. It is a simple, curiously pristine world. The cattle that graze here seem not to have had much experience with hikers. They stare at you with their big, brown eyes framed by lush, almost sexy, eyelashes until you are practically upon them. They then turn and lumber away, dragging their heavy shadows behind them like suitcases.

In contrast to mountainous areas which encourage pockets of diversity, these rolling hills seem to create uniformity. Except for an occasional hawk or an occasional hiker, solitary forms are rare. Instead, virtually everything you see appears in great number: herds of cattle, swarms of insects, colonies of ground squirrels, flocks of blackbirds, and millions of blades of grass. This is a simple environment, an environment of repetition—a bit, one imagines, like the great plains must have been.

Probably the best time to visit Tassajara is during the late spring, after the grasses have bolted to seed, outracing the efforts of the cattle to keep them mowed down. I love to sit on a hillside amidst the wildflowers—Chinese houses, owl's clover, vetch, brodiaea, mustard, and others—and watch the wind swirling and roiling the tall meadow grasses. The grasses dance wildly, bowing and curtsying to one another, then fighting and dueling, then suddenly pulling all together in one direction. These grasslands are like a canvas upon which the winds, usually invisible, can make themselves known, and I feel myself to be in a museum of the wind, the exhibits changing from one second to the next.

I do not want to oversell anyone on the charms of Tassajara. This is, as I have said, mainly a small piece of ordinary land. Yet we live in such curious and paradoxical times, that the "ordinary" is in danger of disappearing, especially here. Originally part of Camp Parks, the military base which lies to the north and west of the park, these 450 acres were declared "surplus military property" in the early 1970s and turned over to the East Bay Regional Park District. The military, however, is currently thinking about reactivating Camp Parks, and it has made moves to take back this open space area. The Park District is resisting the effort, but unless more people visit the area, absorb its flavor, and become part of the effort to protect it, I'm afraid this pure, open grassland will once again be fenced off from public access and be used for drills and gunnery practice. If that should come to pass, we will have lost still another chance to experience the quiet pleasures and almost forgotten beauty of the ordinary.

Directions: From Highway 580, exit at Tassajara Creek Rd. in Pleasanton. The park entrance is 1.6 miles north of the freeway along Tassajara Creek Rd.

Tilden/Wildcat

Topographically, Tilden Regional Park (2,078 acres) and Wildcat Canyon Regional Park (2,420 acres) are almost twins. They lie adjacent to each other, Tilden at the head of the canyon formed by Wildcat Creek, Wildcat just downstream. They are both fundamentally broad valleys bounded by the Berkeley Hills to the west and San Pablo Ridge to the east.

Yet, as sometimes happens with twins, Wildcat and Tilden have gone separate ways. Tilden is penetrated by paved roadways which carry thousands of motorists to the Environmental Education Center, the Little Farm, the golf course, the artificially-created Lake Anza with its popular beach, the Botanic Garden, the miniature train, the merry-go-round, the live pony rides, and so on. Wildcat, on the other hand, has remained a rural backwater. There are no paved roads within it, no instant, easy access to its grassy hillsides. Only a few people hike or jog along its fire roads, look into its open meadows and oak-bay forests, or visit its almost secret side canyons.

Cattle (excluded from Tilden by fences and cattle guards) still greatly outnumber humans in Wildcat Canyon Regional Park, as they have without interruption for over a century-and-a-half. The breeds of cattle, however, have changed. In pre-Gold Rush days, Spanish longhorns could be found grazing these hills and meadows. Wildcat Canyon was then known as Arroyo Chico (Little Canyon), a small part of the immense Rancho El Sobrante. Yankee ships would dock in the Bay, and a clerk would be dispatched to negotiate with Juan José Castro, owner of Rancho El Sobrante, for hides and tallow. Castro would then send his *vaqueros* into this remote canyon to round up the semi-wild cattle.

By the end of the nineteenth century, the longhorns had been totally replaced by dairy cattle, owned by small, independent farmers who supplied milk to the East Bay communities. Many of the geographical features in Wildcat Canyon (Conlon Trail, Mezue Trail, Havey Canyon) carry the names of the dairy farmers who once had ranches and raised their families here. The only physical remains of this lost era are a few scattered sites where houses and barns once stood. Now almost entirely reabsorbed by the land, their locations are betrayed only by a few subtle, sometimes poignant signs: a rose bush, a broken retaining wall, or perhaps a weathered plank, half buried, to which a fragment of a rusty hinge is still attached.

In Tilden, on the other hand, the human presence is very much in the forefront. In fact, no matter what day of the week you visit Tilden, it always seems to be Sunday afternoon. There is a permanent holiday spirit to this park. People wander along the hiking trails and over the hills, coming every day to walk their dogs, jog, or just stretch their minds—the rustic equivalents of *boulevardiers* you find strolling about in a big city. Families picnic in the flowering meadows. Young Berkeleyites with guitars head up the slopes. Some people get only as far as the creek bed a few feet from their picnic tables, while others spend the whole day hiking high into the hills.

The "attractions" in Tilden are mostly concentrated along the valley floor. Personally, I prefer wild land to be left alone, but over the years whenever my various kids have pleaded with me for "something special," as often as not we head for Tilden. And we have always had a fine time. For the kids there is an antique merry-go-round with hand-carved horses and an organ cranking out raunchy, spirited music—music loaded with nostalgia and vitality. There are also pony rides and a miniature train pulled by a genuine steam locomotive. At the Little Farm, goats, cows, sheep, donkeys, and more—a full cast of farm animals—loaf around a miniature barn. The Environmental

Education Center offers exhibits and naturalist programs.

Other attractions of Tilden include Lake Anza (see page 148) where one can swim and Jewel Lake, a big duck pond with a self-guiding nature trail. Tilden also offers horseback riding (private stables outside the park can rent you a horse), tennis courts, an 18-hole golf course, dozens of picnic sites, and the Brazil Building which can be reserved for meetings or parties. At the Botanic Garden, cactuses from the Mojave Desert rub shoulders with flowers from the coastal bluffs, and pines from the Channel Islands meet oaks from the Oregon border. The diverse plant life of the Botanic Garden has attracted a wide variety of birds who (like us) hop happily from one environment to the next without having to migrate more than a few feet at a time.

In addition to the attractions, Tilden has ample land to hike through. There are several different kinds of forests here: the willow thickets alongside water, the thick oak-bay forests of the canyons and valleys, areas of Monterey pine which were planted long ago, and extensive forests of eucalyptus—trees as hard as marble and as straight as masts. Each spring, deer bring their wobbly, freshly-licked fawns out of these forests to feed timidly on the fringes. Jays scold and complain—ordinary jays, yet as exotic and striking as Aztec gods. Quail, plump and ma-tronly, burst like firecrackers each spring into trails of scurrying chicks.

Outside the forests are the vast expanses of grassland and the patches of brush. After every rain dozens of little brooks come out of hiding to play upon the meadows. They dance, bounce, and twinkle, as if to flirt with their brainless taskmaster, gravity. And we laugh along with the brooks, because we know that no matter how hard gravity tries the brooks will be born again, again, and still again with each succeeding rain.

Tilden Park was named after Charles Lee Tilden, the first president of the Park District's Board of Directors. The board meetings often took place in Tilden's home, and in those early years (the 1930s) he even loaned the District money out of his pocket to cover expenses.

The land has had a varied history. Like Wildcat Canyon Regional Park, it too was grazed by longhorns and settled by dairy farmers. There was once a quarry and a slaugh-terhouse here. During the Depression, WPA crews built many of the roads, buildings, and trails, as well as the golf course. And during the Second World War over 2,000 soldiers were stationed here, and throughout the euca-lyptus forests you can still find remains of the foxholes they dug.

Tilden, in other words, is hardly a wilderness. Much of the land has been given over to artificial lakes, irrigated lawns, groves of exotic trees, carnival-like attractons, and the paved roads that crisscross the park. This is where I have brought my three children to feed their first ducks, see their first goat, and ride their first horse. Friends have gotten married here, and I have been guest at—or host to—dozens of picnics from one end of the park to the other. No other piece of public land has become so intertwined with my life, or with the lives of so many other East Bay residents. Yet for all our involvement and for all the alterations we have brought, we have only to wander a few yards away from the picnic tables, the pony rides, or the paved roadways to find the wildness, freedom, and spaciousness that these hills and valleys can still offer. For many of us who live in nearby cities, the repeated and casual contact we have had with Tilden and Wildcat over the years has helped keep alive a wildness, freedom, and spaciousness within us too.

Directions: From Highway 580 take the Fish Ranch Rd. exit just east of the Caldecott Tunnel. Follow Fish Ranch Rd. uphill to Grizzly Peak Blvd. and turn right toward Tilden Park.

The northern end of Tilden can also be reached in the following manner. From Highway 80 (the East Shore Freeway) take the University Ave. exit into Berkeley. At the end of University Ave., turn left on Oxford St. and proceed to Rose St. Turn right on Rose one block to Spruce St., take a left, and follow Spruce steadily up the hill to Grizzly Peak Blvd. Cross Grizzly Peak Blvd. and turn immediately left onto Canon Dr. and into Tilden.

Wildcat Canyon can be reached by taking the Amador St./ Solano Ave. exit off Highway 80 in Richmond and following Amador St. to McBryde Ave. Follow McBryde east to Alvarado Park and the staging area.

See Maps N and O.

BAY AND DELTA

 The San Francisco Bay and Delta area has been one of the best-kept secrets in the state. Juan Cabrillo, the first European to explore the California coast in 1543, missed the Golden Gate completely, sailing right past the one narrow opening to the Bay. And for the next two centuries, explorers, merchantmen, and pirates continued to ply the coast without ever suspecting the presence of this vast body of water. The Bay remained hidden until 1769 when Gaspar de Portolá, marching northward from Monterey with more important things on his mind, stumbled upon it accidentally.

Despite Portolá, the Bay and Delta are still largely undiscovered. We are the modern-day explorers, merchantmen, and pirates who speed by these waters on freeways, speed over them on bridges, and speed under them on BART trains. We catch glimpses of an egret or a cordgrass marsh by looking between factories while on our way to somewhere else. Sadly, the Bay and Delta have become like movie stars or great public figures: everyone knows about them, the newspapers continually feature them, but very few are really intimate with them.

Yet (despite all we have done and neglected to do) the Bay and Delta are still alive and kicking, teeming with wildlife, as free and wild as the cries of their seagulls. You can rediscover them by walking along beaches, tramping through marshes, sitting quietly under sea bluffs, or fishing from piers at the following East Bay Regional Parks. . . .

Antioch Shoreline

Antioch Regional Shoreline is a tiny, 7-acre park just east of the town of Antioch. Although it has a few picnic tables and a small beach, its main draw is a 546-foot concrete fishing pier that juts out into the San Joaquin River. Broad wooden rails guarding the edge of the pier are sloped inward at just the right angle so that people who are fishing can lean easily against them for hours on end. Which indeed they do! Antioch Pier is open 24 hours a day, and when the fish are running strong you can find people leaning against the rails around the clock.

And what a variety of people they are! Infants and elderly; men and women; white, black, Hispanic, and Asian. Some of the Asians, of Chinese descent, have deep California roots, their ancestors having settled here during the Gold Rush era. Others are from Laos, Thailand, and elsewhere in Southeast Asia, immigrants from poverty and political tragedy, who have arrived in America within the last decade.

On a good fishing day you can find over a hundred people leaning against the rails at Antioch Pier. Join them sometime. As many as a dozen radios or tape decks are playing simultaneously—all with different music—but don't let that chase you away. So wide is the view and so steady the wind that although you are surrounded by people you paradoxically feel yourself to be quietly, even comfortably, alone.

Although Antioch Pier is a relatively new facility, it stands on pilings that are over fifty years old. These pilings supported the original Antioch Bridge, built in 1925 in the infancy of the automobile age. The first highway span in the Bay Area, this drawbridge with its two narrow lanes quickly proved inadequate. Automobile traffic would be backed up for miles behind heavy vehicles that were limited to speeds of 15 mph. To make matters worse, the bridge had to be lifted an average of three times daily to allow ships to pass on their way to and from Stockton. For ocean-going ships it was a tight squeeze through the undersized bridge—especially on foggy nights. When in 1970 a ship smashed the bridge, jamming it into an open position for four months, the decision was made to construct a new bridge. The new bridge now soars into the air just west of the old bridge, which was torn down. Some of its pilings, however, were left embedded in the river bottom to support the present fishing pier.

The fishing is good here for catfish, sturgeon, and especially striped bass. Like salmon, the striped bass generally lives its adult life in salt water and returns to fresh water to spawn. Large (a thirty-pound striper is not uncommon), beautifully proportioned, and plentiful, the striped bass—while at home in the Bay Area—is not native. Stripers were introduced to California waters in 1879 by a man named Livingston Stone, who scooped 162 fingerlings—most of them 1½ to 3 inches long—from the Navesink River in New Jersey. He put the fish into milk cans, brought them west by rail, and dumped them into the Carquinez Straits. Shortly thereafter a second plant of 300 fish was obtained from the Shrewsbury River in New Jersey, and they were released in Suisun Bay near Benicia.

The introduction was an astounding success. In 1880, only one year after the fish were released, fishermen reported catching stripers. A fish weighing seventeen pounds was taken in 1883. Striped bass appeared regularly in local markets by 1885, and by 1888 commercial fishermen were seeking them out. By the turn of the century, a mere twenty years after their release from milk cans, the commercial catch of striped bass exceeded 1,250,000 pounds.

Thus anglers, many of them recent immigrants, stand on a recently constructed pier and fish for a recently transplanted fish. The mind boggles at how fast things have changed in the Bay Area. Yet the feeling you have as you lean against the rails at Antioch Pier is not of recent upheavals, but—quite the contrary—of something timeless and grand. The cool air from the coast flows toward the warm inland valleys, creating the prevailing winds that have swept eastward across the Delta for the last geological age. The broad San Joaquin River flows mightily from the Sierra snowbeds as it has done for thousands of years. The nibbling on the hook at the end of your fishing line awakens an impulse that seems as old as our species. I find it a source of deep comfort that you can come to this area of great and recent change and leave nourished and strengthened by contact with some of the most ancient, permanent forces of nature.

Directions: Take Highway 4 east to the Wilbur Ave. off ramp, just before the Antioch Bridge. Make a left onto Bridgehead Rd., which leads to the park.

Brooks Island

Ever since I moved to the Bay Area, I have felt drawn toward Brooks Island. I remember, even from my first months here, scanning the Bay from places in the Berkeley Hills. Invariably, like a bird returning to its nest, my gaze would fall longingly onto Brooks Island, just offshore from Richmond. It looked perfect and serene, a rounded hill of land rising up out of the blue waters. It seemed just the right size for an island: small enough to be encompassed in a single glance, large enough to suggest unanswered questions and unsolved mysteries. Through the years I gazed often at the island, examining its contours, wondering about its past and present, hoping for a personal introduction to its charms.

I inquired about visiting the island in the early 1970s. The story I heard was scarcely believable. Brooks Island, I was told, was controlled by a private pheasant-hunting club. Its members—who included Bing Crosby, "Trader Vic," and other notables—released incubator-bred pheasants onto the island, where a resident caretaker supplied the birds with feed and water. Periodically the notables would boat out to their island for a day of "pheasant hunting." The caretaker was, according to an often-repeated rumor, extremely hostile to anyone who tried to trespass.

Since I could not visit the island (I doubt whether Bing and Vic would have let me join their club) I contented myself with reading what I could about it. Brooks Island, I learned, is a very young island. Geologically it is one of the Potrero Hills—a chain of ground-down mountains still visible on the Richmond shore. About 14,000 years ago (yesterday in geological time) the rising waters of the Bay began to cut it off from the rest of the hills and make it into an island. Until the recent dredging of a deep-water channel, however, it was separated from the mainland only by a broad, swampy area.

For many centuries Indian people crossed the swampy area, probably to gather birds' eggs, collect mussels, or catch fish along the shores. Between three and four thousand years ago they established a small but (from the evidence of kitchen middens) thriving village here.

Little else is known about the early history of Brooks Island. Even its name, which began to appear on maps as early as 1850, is a mystery. Its recorded history begins in the 1870s when Luccas and Dominica Gargurevich, Yugoslavian immigrants, settled here. As we know from the reminiscences of Anton, one of their nine children who were born on the island, the family planted grapevines and fruit trees, raised goats, chickens, cows, and hogs, and had at one time three fishing boats.

In 1886 the Morgan Oyster Company built offshore oyster beds here, raising and selling oysters until 1909 when the increasing pollution of the Bay made oystering impossible. Also, from the 1870s through the 1930s quarrying was a big part of Brooks Island history. Hillsides were gouged, and the rocks—after being pounded and crushed—were loaded into ore cars which hauled them a short way to piers on the north and south sides of the island to be put onto waiting barges.

During this century the island has changed ownership many times. Some of the owners had ambitious plans. An airport, a factory complex, and a container port were among the schemes proposed. But miraculously, the island escaped various forms of gross industrial development, and settled instead for the more genteel ignominy of being the site of a pheasant-hunting club.

The "liberation" of Brooks Island was a long time in coming. The island was purchased by the East Bay Regional Park District in 1969, but its situation did not immediately improve. Without water or sanitation facilities, without a pier at which tour boats could dock, and with no way of preserving Indian shell mounds and other natural sites from vandals, the Park District renewed the lease of the pheasant-hunting club under the provision that the club would continue to provide a resident caretaker to protect the island against vandalism.

In January, 1983, I got special permission from the East Bay Regional Park district to visit the island, and on a clear, calm day I canoed across the channel from the Richmond Yacht Club. After years of fantasy, I was not prepared for what I felt when I first set foot on the island. Exultation? Hardly. What I felt, frankly, was disappointment.

Brooks Island, when seen from afar against the jumbled and congested Richmond shoreline, looked utterly sweet and idyllic. Seen close up, however, it was little more than an ordinary East Bay hill, only forty-five acres in size and a squat 165 feet above sea level at its highest point. I had been told that the island had varieties of plants that are relatively rare today—plants that are more typical of the pre-European California grasslands. But in my first scanning, what I noticed were largely common grasses, flowers, and brush. If this land were transposed to the middle of Tilden Park, I would probably never notice it, but might very well continue along the trail to someplace more interesting.

I wandered over the grass and brush-covered hillside to examine the plant life more closely. There seemed to be more native bunchgrasses than usual, but other than that the plants I saw were among the most common of all Bay Area species: lupine, checker flower, balsam root, soap

plant, wild hyacinth, etc. I looked more closely to see if I could find some oddity among the plants, a subspecies or perhaps genotype that would be endemic to this island, but I couldn't. Indeed, the plants here seemed to be even more ordinary-looking than those on the mainland, their leaves better formed, their shapes more nearly symmetrical.

I strolled into a grove of buckeye trees—the only trees that grow on the island other than some small willows and a few elderberry bushes. It had much the feeling of buckeye groves anywhere—quiet and still, as if the crooked trunks of the trees were bars of a cage that excluded winds and other disturbances from the grove. In fact the grove seemed even more still than groves elsewhere, perhaps because of the clusters of buckeye nuts that lay beneath the trees, gathered into little depressions, reminding me of fruit in a bowl in a still-life painting.

When I came back out into the open, I was annoyed to find what I thought were bicycle tracks in the grass—long, straight lines that went across the meadow. Who in the world would be riding a bicycle here, I wondered. But on looking more closely I discovered that the tracks were tunnels made by meadow mice (or voles), the most common mammal in the Bay Area. The grassland was indeed laced with such tunnels and runways, some of them typically zig-zagging from rock to bush to fallen log, others remarkably straight.

At the top of the hill I looked over the Bay. It was still calm, the thick swells moving gently toward the island, rolled out, it seemed, by an unseen, giant rolling pin. It was calm, peaceful, irresistibly sleep-inducing. I lay down on the hilltop and closed my eyes.

The dull, distant thumping of a pile driver on the Richmond shore woke me up. The winds had picked up significantly, and the water responded by changing color and kicking up whitecaps. My mind was also kicking up whitecaps of its own—scattered and excited thoughts. Why were the plants so perfectly formed that they might almost have been "specimen" plants? Why were these nuts lying on the ground unmoved since they dropped from the trees weeks and months before? Why were so many mouse tunnels curiously and atypically straight? There was a mystery here that did indeed make this island very different from the mainland.

I headed back to the shoreline to discuss it with the new caretaker. A professional zoologist, he confirmed what I had begun to suspect. Brooks Island, like many islands the world over, is poor in animal life. It lacks rabbits and deer, for example, that would ordinarily browse back many of the plants, thus leaving them ragged. It lacks squirrels that would ordinarily distribute the buckeye nuts throughout the hillside. There are no foxes, coyotes, bobcats, or weasels to make the mice fearful and force them into building short, zig-zagging tunnels and runways.

As a matter of fact, the caretaker himself was here to study the population dynamics of the common meadow mouse. On an island without major predators, he could watch mouse behavior in an almost pure, almost laboratory setting. Like their near relatives, the lemmings, meadow mice have periodic population explosions and crashes. Here, with a minimum of interference from predators or competing mammals, he could see how the population peaks and dips, how it regulates itself because of internal checks and balances, and how it responds to the carrying capacity of the land. As he talked, I forgot about foxes, bobcats, and other animals I usually hope to see when I'm outdoors; meadow mice now seemed like the most fascinating animals in the world.

It was getting late in the afternoon and the winds were picking up. I could find no remains whatever of the vineyards and fruit trees planted by Luccas Gargurevich a century before. On the south side of the island I investigated a surreal landscape of ponds, cliffs, benches, scarps, and old pilings left behind by the quarrying operations. From a freshwater quarry pond, frogs and redwinged blackbirds piped among the reeds, and ducks dabbled in the water—peaceful heirs of past violence to the land. I

walked along the shoreline, strewn with rubble and flotsam. A small flock of sandpipers peeped and skittered
nervously through a saltwater marsh. A cormorant lifted
off an old piling. I was reminded of a description left
behind by Sam and Nellie Blanford, caretakers of the
island from 1967 through 1971:

> You ain't seen or heard nothing yet 'til you listen to wild
> birds singing or small shorebirds weaving their marvelous
> flight patterns. . . . Long rows of avocets, walking and
> swinging their long bills from side to side in perfect unison,
> search the shallow water for marine life. We talked to the
> birds and the animals and the plants, not because we were
> lonesome but because we liked to. And we believe, in some
> small way, they answered. Crazy you say? Such a nice
> crazy, though, and we were so happy. . . .

A seagull laughed overhead. I laughed, too. I had come
to the island, hopeless fool that I am, searching for the
exotic and the romantic. I left the island calmed and
charmed once again by the singular sweetness and beauty
of the "commonplace."

What is the future for Brooks Island? As of spring, 1987,
the lease of the pheasant-hunting club expired. But there
are still problems to be worked out before a ferry service
can be inaugurated and the island opened to the public.
There is no suitable landing for boats, so a pier will have to
be rebuilt and extended, and significant dredging will have
to be undertaken. Also, botanists fear that the island's
vegetation will get trampled with too much visitation,
while archaeologists are concerned with protecting the
Indian burial sites. Consequently, even when Brooks
Island is opened to the public, it will probably be on a
limited, reservation-only basis.

So it looks like Brooks Island, despite its ordinariness,
may yet remain a somewhat exclusive club. Fortunately, it
will be a club which anyone can join—even the likes of
Bing and Vic.

Brooks Island is not officially open to the public.

Browns Island

Browns Island, in the channel of the San Joaquin River, opposite the city of Pittsburg, offers what is very likely the worst hiking available anywhere in the Bay Area. If you encircle the island on a boat, searching for a place to land, you will see along its shore only a ten-foot tall, nearly impenetrable wall of the densest vegetation—tule, cattail, and other reeds that choke most of the island's 595 acres. Beach the boat and plunge into the wall, and within seconds the vegetation swallows you up. Without trails or fire roads—the island has none—you find yourself trapped in a prison of green bars. You cannot see more than a few feet in any direction. Previous generations of tule and cattails have fallen and now lay in deep, often breast-high tangles. They are so thickly matted that you cannot walk on solid ground and push your way through them. But they are so springy and loose that you cannot walk on top of them either. With your feet, knees, and waist in shackles, every step forward is a momentous effort.

Let me describe in greater detail what it is like to move forward a few feet. From a standing position—itself quite an achievement here—you try thrusting one leg in front of you; your foot burrows its way through the tangles of tule until it comes to rest on a knot of stems dense enough to support weight. You then—just as you have been doing since the age of nine or ten months—swing the second leg forward, past the first leg, and plunge it, too, into the tangles. Now as you begin to lift the rearmost foot, you discover a serious design flaw in the human anatomy: namely, that your foot juts out from your leg at a right angle. As you try to draw it up and out of the tangles, several tons of intermatted tule and cattail stems get caught in the offending right angle. So you try backing up to extricate the rearmost foot, thereby twisting the forward foot and entangling it in its own trap of tule and cattail stems. At this point there is nothing to do except collapse into a graceless (and physically painful) sitting position, while you reach down with your hands into the sea of stems, trying to free one or the other foot, while at the same time trying to keep your head from getting caught in the tule tangles also.

Since walking is hopeless, you revert to other motions: crawling, rolling, clawing, sometimes almost swimming. As you move forward on the dense mattress of stems you long for *terra firma*—until the rare time when your foot *does* reach below the tangle of stems. Now you discover that the hoped-for solid ground is totally waterlogged, more or less the consistency of pudding. When the God of the Old Testament divided the seas from the lands, he apparently overlooked Browns Island. You wish that you, too, had overlooked Browns Island.

But you struggle onward. Or is it onward? After a while the suspicion seizes you that you are travelling in a circle. You try to claw your way above the tule stems to catch a glimpse of a distant mountain or city or smoke stack that might help orient you. But while you "swim" toward the sky, the tangles beneath you periodically collapse, plunging you—sometimes head first—back into the prison of tule and the pudding of land.

Is this the worst? Not at all. I saved the "crowning glory" of Browns Island for last. Every inch of the tules and cattails is covered with aphids, who mindlessly spend the entire summer exuding a thick, sticky liquid the texture of honey, that coats everything you touch. At one point on an excursion to Browns Island, I felt that I knew exactly how a fly must feel when caught in a spider's web. It's that dreadful!

Fortunately, there is an alternative trail system on Browns Island. Sloughs run deep into its center, branching out, rejoining each other, widening into sizeable lakes, narrowing into the thinnest of winding channels. These are the veins, arteries, and capillaries that feed the island's vegetation—swelling and heaving, attaining a moment of quiescent pause, then draining according to the rhythm of the tides—to form a trail system that is organic, alive, always changing, always surprising.

I first visited these sloughs with my oldest son, Reuben, when he was fifteen. We put our canoe in at the launching ramp next to the Pittsburg Marina and paddled in the morning calm across the open expanse of water to the southern shore of the island. We then rounded the island to its northern shore and entered the sloughs. Unlike ordinary trail systems, which are planned, built, and maintained by people, these sloughs are natural, as mysterious, complex, and organic as a network of roots or nerves. In their widenings, narrowings, and twistings they follow laws outside human ken. We moved through this ancient system of waterways as guests, diminished by the complexity, startled and humbled by the constant surprise. We paddled deeper and deeper into the island. Out of a lake ducks rose up, flew away, and settled into the distant reeds, leaving us utterly alone. We probed channels scarcely wider than the canoe, with the reeds brushing both sides of the canoe and rising high above us. We felt curiously like a needle entering into fabric, burrowing deeper and deeper, until—with what surprise!—we emerged into another widening, another lake, yet one more world.

As time passed, we got lost in the sloughs, so labyrinthine are their branchings, so without landmark in that flat, swampy land. For many hours we struggled to find our way out, working always against the flow of the water which was now moving in on a rising tide. As afternoon progressed, winds came up. Paddling was difficult, and for a while I was convinced that we would have to spend the night on Browns Island, shivering and cramped in the canoe. Finally, without warning, as we rounded a bend in a channel, open water lay before us. It was a terrifying sight.

What had been calm and clear during the morning was now gray and choppy, wild with whitecaps. The wind howled. We tried to move the canoe into open water, but could make no headway. Water splashed into the canoe, and as we tried to bail it out the waves pushed us against the shore of the island. We jumped out, hauled the boat into the reeds, and stood at the shore—like cartoon figures on a desert island—waving our shirts at the one passing motorboat (other boats had obviously put in long ago). As the motorboat pulled close to the land to pick us up, its propeller choked with tule stems and its motor went dead. It too was now a piece of flotsam, tossed by the seas and the wind. The owner of the boat panicked: "We're gonna lose the boat, we're gonna die. Jesus, we're gonna lose the boat. Mother of God, we're gonna die. Jesus help us, we're gonna die." He screamed over the winds in a helpless terror.

Fortunately, we didn't lose the boat, nor did we die. We waded into the water to hold the boat from the shore, cleaned out its propeller, got the motor started again, and headed back through the wind to Pittsburg. A few days later I returned, hired someone with a launch to take me to the island, attached a line to the canoe, and towed it back.

After an experience such as this, there was, of course, only one thing to do. Reuben and I returned to Browns Island later in the year, on a clear, sunny, Indian summer day in early October, when the entire Bay Area was windless and (according to the weather forecast) would remain windless. We put in again at the launching ramp near the Pittsburg Marina, paddled across the now glassy waters, and entered the sloughs. The tules that lined the channels were now slightly browned in the fall, in places seemingly bundled together almost like sheaves of wheat. Their reflections shimmered in the water, giving us the feeling that we had entered an Impressionist painting. We paddled along the major sloughs and poked into the narrowest of channels, sometimes placing our paddles inside the canoe and pulling ourselves by hand through the tules that grew thickly on either side, probing the island with a sense of first exploration and unfolding intimacy. The water, even at its widest, was almost without a ripple. Asters, vetches, and other flowers lined the banks. Blackberry vines were laden with drooping, wet, sweet berries. The air was thick and sensual, so warm and so comfortable that the body lost all sense of its own boundaries. Hours passed and we scarcely spoke. I watched Reuben's strong, young back as we worked the canoe through the channels with a quiet teamwork developed over years of canoeing and being together. We got back easily and uneventfully. We had little to say. It was a day of utter bliss.

I hesitate to recommend the exploration of these channels to others. I have spent only two days on Browns Island, and I wouldn't have swapped either of those days for six months of ordinary living. Yet one of those days was dangerous, indeed life-threatening. So while I am pleased to describe my exploration of these sloughs, I am reluctant to recommend the experience to others. Perhaps there will be a few hardy souls, knowledgeable about boating and well-equipped for emergencies, who will try it; I hope others will be content to experience it through the pages of this book.

Clearly, the East Bay Regional Park District is not managing Browns Island for its recreation potential. In fact, it is not really managing Browns Island at all, but rather leaving it very much alone. And for good reason. This is one of the few areas left in the Delta that is thoroughly natural, never having been altered by levees, drained, or used for agriculture. Browns Island is a remnant of a marshland that once covered 750,000 acres—over 1,000 square miles—and is consequently highly valued by ecologists and biologists. John Thomas Howell, formerly curator of the California Academy of Sciences, declared this island to be a "botanist's paradise," claiming that nowhere else in the Delta region do so many rare and potentially endangered marsh plants grow in such undisturbed circumstance. Among the plants indigenous to the Delta marshes that grow on Browns Island are tule pea (*Lathyrus jepsonii*), Bolander's water hemlock (*Cicuta bolanderi*), Harkness coyote thistle (*Eryngium harknessii*), Mason's lilaeopsis (*Lilaeopsis masonii*), Suisun aster (*Aster chilensis* var. *lentus*), and marsh gumweed (*Grindelia paludosa*).

The importance of protecting this environment is obvious, and I passionately hope that this botanical treasure house can be preserved forever, a permanent living museum of Delta vegetation and Delta mood. Yet while I talk (in all sincerity) about "forever" and "permanence," I cannot shake off a deep feeling that it is *impermanence* that gives Browns Island its extraordinary tone and character.

Unlike other East Bay land, where hills, rocks, and large trees seem to have been in place for hundreds of years, everything on Browns Island seems to be in a state of constant flux, just "passing through," as it were. The winds that so constantly sweep over the island are flowing from the ocean toward the Central Valley. The waters that wash through the channels and percolate through the tules come from the Sierra snow melt, or are flushed back and forth by ocean tides. The salmon that nose their way through the sloughs are on their way to spawning grounds in the cold mountain streams. The thousands of geese and ducks that flock on Browns Island's lakes—pintails, mallards, ruddy ducks, gadwalls, scoters, teal, bafflehead, goldeneyes, white-fronted geese, lesser snow geese, and wood ducks—are merely visiting, migrants from the tundras of Canada, Alaska, and even Siberia. The soil that comprises the island is silt, washed down from the Sierra, pausing here briefly on its slow geological journey toward the Bay.

So fragile and tentative is this island, that if I were to invent a language to describe it, it would be a language without nouns—a language of verbs, adjectives, and adverbs—a language that would refer not to concrete "things," but rather to the nuances of tone, coloration, and change. Less than solid, Browns Island seems so shifting and unsubstantial that it appears more like a dream of land than land itself.

Our paddles dip into the water as we gently draw the canoe around another bend in the channel and enter a large, amazingly still lake. There is no wind or water current. The water is unruffled and the tule along the bank is as motionless as in a painting. Movement stops, time stops, and we are floating in a pool of myth. It is here that I can almost see the cradle of Moses among the bulrushes. It is here that I can almost hear the cries of the Babylonian infant, Gilgamesh, among the reeds. It is here that I can almost feel the presence of Turtle Old Man and Pehe-ipe ("Father of the Secret Society") of whom the Central Valley Maidu told, floating on a moss-covered raft in the ancient waters, long before World-Initiate arrived to bring the present world into being.

Park administrators are preserving Browns Island primarily as a botanical remnant of a marshland that once extended throughout the Delta for hundreds of square miles. In the process they are preserving something else: a spiritual and mythic remnant of places that have occupied a huge part of the human consciousness for thousands of years—places that are now almost totally inaccessible except in dreams, in literature, or (if you are lucky) in a day of idyllic paddling through the sloughs of Browns Island.

Browns Island is not officially open to the public.

Crown Beach

Robert Crown Memorial Beach—better known as Alameda Beach—is a skinny stretch of sand and rock that runs
two-and-a-half miles along the Bay at Alameda. There is
swimming, sun-bathing, shell collecting, bird watching,
and people watching here. Professional and amateur
athletes run through the sand to build muscles—and apparently nothing builds muscles quite like running through
the sand. Scores of people come to fly kites in the offshore
winds. The warm water and light morning breezes that
blow toward land (not out into the Bay) make Alameda
Beach especially good for beginning sailboarders. You can
bring your own, or rent a sailboard from a private company that shows up on the beach throughout much of the
spring, summer, and fall. The company also offers lessons.

I truly enjoy Alameda Beach, but I do not want to pretend
for a moment that it is a tropical paradise. Alameda Beach is
an urban beach in a heavily urban area. Housing developments run down to the borders of the beach. Jets roar
overhead. Plastic spoons and scrap wood dumped into the
Bay at other places float onto the shore and must be cleaned
up. Alameda Beach is very much part of the Bay Area. It has
all the noise and pollution which we all know very well. But
it also has a lot of the beauty and drama of the Bay which we
too often ignore. There is tide and wind and the sun. There's
a big sense of time that you get from spending a day at the
beach, and a big sense of scale that you feel from looking
across the Bay to the hazy mountains in the distance. Alameda Beach is a good place to get in touch with the rhythms
of the Bay—and perhaps in the process of sun-bathing and
surf watching, with the rhythms of your own consciousness
as well.

You'd never guess it at first glance, but Alameda Beach is

rich in wildlife. The wildlife is mostly underground. It consists of clams, oysters, many kinds of worms, barnacles, shrimps, crabs, creatures that burrow in the sand, and creatures that cling to rocks. If you think human beings have strange habits, just consider. At Alameda Beach there are oysters that change sex every year (male one year, female the next). There are flatworms that can digest their internal organs in times of starvation and grow new ones later on. Alameda Beach has many incredible forms of life which you can see, study, and handle. There are strange, marvelous happenings in the mud and under the rocks. Lift a rock and see what scurries out. Bring a magnifying glass to study and contemplate these exotic little animals. But afterwards, as an act of ecological courtesy, replace the rocks in their original positions to keep these creatures' environments intact.

At the southern end of the park is a cordgrass marsh that is set aside as a bird sanctuary. Cordgrass thrives in salty soil and is actually five times as nutritious as wheat. In fact, it is considered to be the most productive type of natural vegetation in North America. When the grass dies and decays, tons of nutrients are released. The ooze of a cordgrass marsh supports an unbelievable concentration of mollusks, crustaceans, and smaller forms of life. This, in turn, is what attracts all those thousands of birds you find here, delicately sliding their long bills into the mud.

Every year Alameda Beach holds a sand castle contest. Kids build sand castles, sand palaces, sand fortresses, and sand cathedrals on the beach. Every year exquisite sand civilizations rise up and flourish briefly until the next high tide.

This reminds me of the history of Alameda Beach.

The first great sand civilization that arose here was that of the Indians who collected oysters and clams along the bayshore. Only the shell mounds further inland are left to remind us of the Indian civilization that was once here.

Then came Neptune Beach which flourished between 1890 and 1939. Neptune Beach was built to rival Copenhagen's Tivoli Gardens. It had a ballroom, swimming pool, skating rink, and theater. The years added a roller coaster, merry-go-round, thrill rides, and honky-tonk, as Neptune Beach became the "Coney Island of the West." Edwin Booth acted here, boxers "Gentleman Jim" Corbett and Bob Fitzsimmons trained here, and Robert Louis Stevenson and Jack London wrote here. But by 1939 the automobile, the Bay Bridge, other amusement parks, and changing tastes drove Neptune Beach into bankruptcy. By now nearly all traces have been obliterated.

The next great sand civilization was the U.S. Maritime Training Center built during the Second World War. The seamen are gone now, but the East Bay Regional Park District still uses the hospital as its naturalists' headquarters and the boat-shaped *Glory of the Sea* training center as a maintenance garage.

Then came the developers who in the early 1950s began to fill the land between the Alameda Lagoon and the present beach. They pumped sand from the bottom of the Bay to fill out the current contours of Alameda Beach.

In 1967 the State of California and the City of Alameda leased the beach to the East Bay Regional Park District. The Park District is the present sand civilization. It has added a bath house, snack bar, and picnic areas. It has planted green lawns, built a day-camp shelter, is nursing along some still puny shade trees, and has assigned a crew to keep the beach clean. Naturally, the East Bay Regional Park District thinks that its hold on Alameda Beach is permanent. So did the other sand civilizations. Today the Bay is beating up against the beach, trying to reclaim the filled-in portions, nibbling at the shorelines, trying relentlessly to gobble up Alameda Beach once more. You can see the signs of the battle all along the beach. The East Bay Regional Park District, however, has enlisted the aid of the U.S. Army Corps of Engineers, which has completed a "demonstration project" to control erosion in the most critical areas. With such steps, the latest sand civilization hopes that it will persevere and continue to serve the thousands of people who, on any warm day, can be found swimming in the water, basking in the sun, playing in the sand, or sailing in the winds of Alameda Beach.

Directions: To reach the Crab Cove Visitor Center from Oakland, take Webster St. (which runs parallel to Broadway two blocks to the east) through the Posey Tube to Alameda. Continue on Webster St. to Central Ave. Turn right onto Central, go one block to McKay Ave., and turn left on McKay to the park entrance. To reach the main part of the beach, turn left on Central, then right at the first light (8th St.) and follow 8th St. to the park entrance.

   For information about naturalist tours or other activities, call 521-6887.

Hayward Shoreline

Hayward Regional Shoreline is huge and it is flat. Incredibly flat! Surveyors have found that the ground surface ranges in elevation from 1.0 to 2.5 feet. Levees that crisscross the area vary from 5.0 to 9.5 feet. One walks through this vast, flat world with a sense of disorientation. Those of us living in cities and driving on highways depend upon having our space divided into lanes, lines, alleys, and blocks. Even those of us who love the outdoors generally hike in areas where hills and trees give us topographic variation by which we define space. But except for some fill areas near the park entrance, at Hayward Regional Shoreline there are no hills, there are no trees. There is an immense, flat land waiting to be discovered, learned about, and perhaps appreciated.

At the moment, Hayward Regional Shoreline is rather difficult to appreciate. It is hardly attractive—at least in any conventional sense of the word. The vegetation is sparse, mostly pickleweed growing along the sides of the levees and on a few Lilliputian rises. The rest is bare mud. But things are changing. Hayward Regional Shoreline is the site of what is now the largest marsh restoration project on the West Coast. Freshwater, brackish water, and salt water marshes—some five hundred acres of them—are currently in the process of being rebuilt.

Old maps show that this area was once a huge and thriving marshland—as was indeed the entire southern part of the Bay. Inland were a series of freshwater ponds that drained into each other. As the fresh water moved toward the Bay it gradually became more and more brackish as it mixed with the salt water. Tules gave way to pickleweed and then cordgrass. Sheltered from the strong ocean currents and from heavy winds, the tidal waters in this part of the Bay are extremely gentle, heaving and ebbing rhythmically, and they encouraged vast expanses of cordgrass marshland that grew without erosion far into the waters of the Bay.

In 1865 a man named Patrizio Marsicano chose this site for the establishment of the American Salt Company. He built dikes on the outermost reaches of the cordgrass marsh to entrap as much salt water as possible. Within the newly created stagnant area he built other dikes and levees to create a series of evaporating ponds. A large windmill was installed to pump the water from one pond to the next.

The American Salt Company harvested salt from this area until 1927, when the land was leased to the Leslie Salt Company. Leslie already owned ample land around the Bay, and the Hayward site was never actively used again, except for a brief period between 1938 and the mid-1940s.

For the last several decades, the Hayward Shoreline has been left unused and thoroughly degraded. Seaward dikes have prevented the tides from bringing fresh salt water into the marsh. Freshwater runoff from the land has been diminished by industrial development on the Hayward flatlands, especially by the construction of the immense sewage treatment facilities of the East Bay Dischargers Authority immediately east of the park.

By the late 1970s the Hayward shoreline was so bleak and naked that it was painful and embarrassing even to look at it. Several governmental agencies banded together to see what could be done. Land was purchased, management plans developed, funds raised, and a new vision set forth.

Yet while it is rather easy to destroy a marsh, rebuilding one is a far more difficult and delicate affair. One cannot simply tear down the various dikes and levees and let the land "go back to nature." The outer dikes have to be breached slowly and systematically to allow the gradual reentry of salt water; otherwise the tides would flood and scour the degraded land. The sides of the levees in particular have to be carefully graded and in some places rip-

rapped to prevent erosion. Islands for ground-nesting birds have to be created to isolate them from humans and feral animals that now have access to the marsh by way of levees. The creation of a freshwater marsh here is particularly difficult since the runoff from the Hayward flatlands has been so altered over the century.

Solving these various problems has demanded far more engineering than one would generally tolerate on "natural" land. The fresh water will be supplied by tapping waste water from the adjacent East Bay Dischargers Authority. This water will be drawn from one pond to the next as part of a purification process, supporting first a freshwater environment, then, as it mixes with the waters of the Bay, a brackish water environment, until finally— after several stages—the water will be released into the Bay. Islands have been planned and built, not just topographically, but right down to what kind of vegetation they will support. On the mud flats and at the lowest elevations of these islands, planners expect the return of cordgrass and the rails and other forms of bird and animal life that flourish in a cordgrass environment. At slightly higher elevations we should see a growth of pickleweed, gumweed, jaumea, and other plants which will in turn provide a habitat for small mammals and nesting areas for the saltmarsh song sparrows, mallards, gadwalls, cinnamon teals, and possibly marsh hawks. At still slightly higher elevations (and we are talking, remember, about differences of a few inches) planners expect more brush, with nesting sites for savannah sparrows and roosts for herons and egrets. Bare spots on the levees and islands will be used by ground-nesting birds such as black-necked stilts, avocets, killdeer, and Forster's terns. There is even a 27-acre site set aside especially to provide an environment suitable for the saltmarsh harvest mouse, an endangered species.

Hayward Regional Shoreline is, in short, a thoroughly engineered environment—as well-planned as a shopping mall. There is, of course, a danger in this. Instead of the beauty and excitement of a natural environment, we may get something that looks as if it were packaged by landscape architects and designers. Yet there is tremendous hope, too. For years "engineering" has been a bad word among environmentalists. The assumption has been that human intervention and planning are bad, done for some narrow and short-term economic gain rather than for the benefit of the natural world. Hayward Regional Shoreline will give us an opportunity to challenge that assumption, to find out whether indeed engineering can become a sensitive tool for the restoration of previously abused land. I hope that this will be the case, and that what is happening at Hayward Regional Shoreline will become a model for restoring thousands of acres of marshland throughout the entire Bay Area. Nor am I alone in that hope. From the moment the outer dikes were breached, the birds began to return. There are now countless sandpipers and other shorebirds stepping over the mudflats, probing and poking for food. As I approach they rise up and fly away. The sound of their wings seems to me a prolonged and hearty applause.

Directions: Take Highway 880 (the Nimitz Freeway) to Hayward and exit at Winton Ave. Head west on Winton to the park gate.

Martinez Shoreline

Martinez Regional Shoreline is a 340-acre park wedged between the town of Martinez and the Carquinez Straits. It has an immense green lawn, fallow fields with weeds and grasses, a swampy area of tule and cattails, plus assorted recreational facilities such as a baseball field, a fishing pier, playgrounds, picnic tables, and bocce (pronounced bott-chee) ball courts.

Martinez Regional Shoreline defies the usual cliches about parks. One cannot say that it is remote, because it isn't; it is the "front yard" of the town of Martinez, within a stone's throw of the city center. Nor can one say that it preserves some vestige of a threatened environment. The truth is that the land the park sits on did not even exist a century ago; it was created in part by land fill, in part by accelerated siltation in the Carquinez Straits. As far as I know, no endangered plant or animal lives in this park. Nor was the park set up to commemorate a historical past. While this area was once the waterfront of Martinez and the scene of a thriving fishing industry, Martinez Regional Shoreline does not really seem to be focused on the past as much as on the future, and for this reason it is one of the most unusual of the Regional Parks.

To appreciate Martinez Regional Shoreline, one must understand something about the town of Martinez. The county seat of Contra Costa County, it is nonetheless a small town. When I first visited here, in the late 1970s, it reminded me strongly of a decaying New England mill town after industry had moved out and much of the younger generation had abandoned it. It seemed poor and rundown, its streets quiet and sad—a town drained of energy, youth, and purpose, with store after store either vacant or occupied by used clothing shops, dated beauty parlors, or marginal furniture stores with perpetual sales on formica dinette sets.

Martinez had not always been so impoverished. During the great salmon runs of the past it was, in fact, proud and prosperous. Millions of king salmon used to crowd through the narrow Straits before fanning out into the Sacramento and San Joaquin River systems to spawn. The salmon were so thick that early travelers claimed that it looked as if one could walk across the Straits on their backs. The Indian villages here were the largest and wealthiest in the Bay Area. The men would paddle their tule boats into the Straits, anchor themselves to pilings driven into the river bed, and set their nets against the flow of salmon. The first Spanish explorer to visit the area described how these fishermen were utterly exhausted from carrying armloads of fish ashore after a successful excursion.

In the late nineteenth century Italian fishermen, mostly of Sicilian descent, continued the tradition. They moored their old-world *feluccas*—fast, narrow, lateen-rigged boats—along Alhambra Creek, and when the winds and tides were favorable, they would lift their gaily colored sails and move into the Straits. They landed the fish at Granger's Wharf, built in 1876 by Dr. John Strentzel—a country physician and orchardist who is better known as John Muir's father-in-law. Two large canneries on shore processed the fish and the canned salmon was then shipped by train and boat to other parts of the country. Sturgeon and later striped bass were also caught in large numbers. In 1882 some 2,500 commercial fishermen were working the Straits. On sunny days their nets were strung along the waterfront to dry, while the men got together to talk or to play an old-world favorite game, bocce ball.

Salmon fishing decreased over the years as parts of the Sacramento and San Joaquin river systems were dammed and degraded; but until 1957 salmon fishing was still a major source of employment for Martinez. In that year, however, state conservation laws were passed that banned all commercial fishing east of the Carquinez Bridge. The canneries closed their doors, and the era of commercial fishing came to an abrupt end. There was nothing to take its place. The wharf area lay abandoned, the canneries deserted, the docks unused, buildings and rail spurs derelict and overgrown. Litter collected. Children were told not to play here. The area was an eyesore, and to those who grew up nearby and could recall its former vigor, it was a heartache.

In the early 1970s members of the community came together to grapple with the problem of their waterfront. Because it had the potential of being a deepwater port, many urged that it be used for heavy industry or for a refinery. Such proposals were rejected, however; the area was too close to the center of town. Other options were suggested. While the waterfront was no longer viable as a commercial fishing harbor, some pointed out, there had always been other values to it. The bocce ball courts still stood, as did a baseball field. The views of the hills and of the Strait were excellent. The docks could be used for sportfishing and boating. The decision was made to turn away from commercial use and toward recreation. It was a difficult and in many ways painful decision for a working-class town desperately in need of a broader tax base and better jobs. There was fierce debate, but eventually a recreation-oriented masterplan was created, and, in conjunction with the East Bay Regional Park District, the area was converted into the park that now stands here.

Pleasure and sportfishing boats pull out of the small marina and into the main channel of the Carquinez Straits. On an old pier, people (many of them recent Asian immigrants) angle for fish. Joggers run along trails that wind through the marshes and around the lawns. A car in the parking lot has its radio turned on, and a flock of coots, with charcoal gray bodies, are waddling across the lawn, ludicrously in time to the music. Families cluster around picnic tables and some of them are tossing bread crumbs to the strange assortment of birds that have gathered around them: seagulls, starlings, geese, domestic ducks, mallards, and pigeons, all mixed together, cooing, peeping, quacking, cawing, and honking as they jostle each other to get at the crumbs.

The bocce ball courts are often crowded on weekends. This was a favorite pastime of Italian fishermen—most of the bocce ball courts in this country are found near waterfronts—because the game could be played with a minimum of equipment while the men were waiting around the docks for nets to dry or winds to change. Today this curiously gentle and slow-paced game, whose origins go back to the Roman Empire, is played by men and women of all ages and ethnic backgrounds—people who are perhaps waiting for a different kind of wind to change. Teams form and play begins. The wooden object ball, the *pallino,* is sent down the smooth, dirt alley. Players then roll heavy metal balls toward the *pallino.* The metal balls travel slowly, weighed down or kept going, it seems, by the curses, best wishes, and devout attention of players and spectators alike.

Martinez Regional Shoreline achieved some minor notice in the press a few years ago when Joe DiMaggio, who was born in Martinez in 1914, returned "home" to dedicate a softball field that had been named after him. In 1981 the United States Championship Bocce Ball Tournament was held here.

For most Bay Area residents, however, Martinez Regional Shoreline is an out-of-the-way, little-known park. Yet paradoxically, there are people throughout the United States who are watching it closely. Along the Atlantic Ocean, the Pacific Ocean, the Gulf of Mexico, and along thousands of miles of riverways are communities whose waterfronts have fallen into disrepair. For them Martinez Regional Shoreline is a bold experiment, perhaps a model to be considered.

Many local government officials and business people see the changes along their waterfront as helping to spur a different kind of development in Martinez. The downtown area is now being restored, and a collection of small, up-scale shops is springing up. Thrift stores are giving way to antique shops and boutiques, donut shops to bakeries and gourmet restaurants. Young people are once again strolling along the sidewalks.

Those of us who have watched similar changes in Berkeley and Oakland may view such development with jaded eyes. But those who knew Martinez just a few years ago as a sad, run-down, deeply depressed city will have to acknowledge that the reinvigoration of the downtown area has brought hope and pride to the people there. It has brought a kind of prosperity and vitality that many feel began with the improvements at Martinez Regional Shoreline.

Directions: Take Highway 680 (north) to the Marina Vista exit, one exit before the Benicia Bridge. Head west on Marina Vista to Ferry St., and turn right on Ferry to the park entrance.

Miller-Knox Shoreline

Miller-Knox Regional Shoreline covers about 260 acres of land on Point Richmond, just south of the Richmond-San Rafael Bridge. In the midst of oil refineries, and with a name more appropriate for a law firm than a regional park (George Miller, a state senator, and John Knox, a state assemblyman, were both helpful in furthering the interests of the East Bay Regional Park District), this is an odd place indeed. In many ways it feels like four totally separate but adjacent parks, each with its own distinct character and group of users.

On the northern end of Miller-Knox is Keller's Beach, a small, lovely semi-circular cove that opens like a bowl toward the Bay. On calm days the waves from the Bay roll gently and steadily to shore. Kids play in the sand or splash in the water. Adults doze on beach blankets, their biggest decision of the afternoon being when to turn over to assure an even tan.

Stretching south from Keller's Beach alongside the bay-shore is a wall of riprap. Seagulls perch upon some of the rocks, their eyes full of smug contentment, their voices full of raucous want. People also sit upon the rocks, some casting their lines out for flounder, perch, striped bass, or other fish, others simply enjoying the view of the Marin shoreline across the Bay.

The third distinct area at Miller-Knox is a 25-acre green lawn with a 6-acre lagoon in the middle. Separated from the shore by a fence, it is of almost golf course proportions. Here and there are clusters of picnic tables around pine trees. Planted recently, the pines are not yet very tall, so sometimes they seem more like guests at the picnic tables than the large shade trees they may some day become.

I spent a day at Miller-Knox in mid-July, once, hoping

to get better acquainted with this huge expanse of lawn. I decided to treat this great, green turfed area with complete respect, to see it as an ecological environment. I would study its flora and describe its fauna and (so I resolved) learn to appreciate their relationships.

I arrive early enough on a Sunday morning, well before picnickers can be expected to appear, and set about trying to identify the grass species. Unfortunately the turfed area was recently mowed, and not only has the grass never gone to seed but each blade is cut in half. I notice, however, some small, low-lying flowers—clovers and trefoils—that have escaped the mower blades, and these are host to a number of bumble bees and honey bees that buzz from flower to flower. The only other fauna are a few songbirds perched in the pine trees and some gophers who have dug their holes around the periphery of the lawn. The wildlife seems rather sparse, to be honest, and I note with irony that the clusters of picnic tables have been given names like Canvas-back, Marsh Hawk, and Pintail—tributes, I suppose, to the memory and image of wildlife, rather than to the flesh-and-blood thing itself.

I linger a bit more on the lawn, trying hard to appreciate it esthetically. It is an environment that will always be green and well-trimmed. The grasses will never go to seed, never turn yellow. It will never mature, never grow old, never change into something else. This lawn is eternal youth, I realize, and from eternal youth there is only one proper response: flight! As quickly as possible I head toward the fourth distinct area of Miller-Knox, the Potrero Hills and Nicholl Knob.

The Potrero Hills are small, scruffy, rounded hills that overlook the park. Rising only a few hundred feet above sea level, scarred by old roads and by gullies that motorcycles once dug into the land, they are now crisscrossed by hiking trails. In mid-July, these hills are golden brown from the dried grasses.

I had always considered the dry, yellow grasses of summer to be "dead," representing a period of dormancy in

California's seasonal cycle. But having fled the bright, green, "living" lawn, I find these hillsides to be alive with the most wondrous vitality and variety. Long stalks of wild oats respond quickly and sensitively to the slightest breeze. Summer flowers—lupines, a seaside daisy, mustards, wild radishes, poppies, fennels, and more—startle the eye. Insects buzz, lumber, or scurry through the profligate tangles of dry grass, flowers, and brush. Swallows dip and dart overhead. Lizards scamper under rocks.

A huge swallowtail butterfly flutters across the trail, and I follow its floppy erratic flight. Another butterfly cuts across my field of vision—a cabbage butterfly, as intensely white as a starched shirt. I follow the bouncing flight of the cabbage butterfly as it swoops down close to a clump of low-growing wild buckwheat flowers. There I notice still other butterflies, tiny ones so small that even with their wings spread they are not much bigger than dimes.

I stoop down to look closer at these tiny butterflies. With their wings open, they show a most marvelous azure color, light at the edges and deepening to an almost fluorescent blue toward the center parts of the body. The tops of the wings are fringed with tiny orange bars. When they fold their wings together, the underparts are a pale white, speckled with darker dots. They remind me of temple dancers as they flutter weightlessly around the "altar" of the buckwheat flowers, sipping the nectar.

Among them I notice another butterfly, like the rest in all details except that the top side, instead of being azure, is a rich chocolate brown and the tiny bars are an even more vivid orange. It too sips nectar, and as it sips one of the blue ones comes closer, their bodies tangle for a moment, and then they separate. I have been watching these diminutive blues (for that is their name) for so long and with such involvement that when a buckeye butterfly flutters low over the buckwheat flowers and casts a shadow over the blues, I recoil in shock at how huge it is.

I continue walking to the top of the hills, wondering about these little butterflies. I am trying my best to think "elevated" thoughts about ecological relationships, but I cannot help wondering what these diminutive, weightless insects feel when they mate. How much passion and longing and joy can such small bodies, such small brains, contain? It is beyond my abilities to imagine this, but it is not beyond my abilities to rejoice that these fragile little animated flower petals can carry on this way right next to one of California's most industrialized areas.

And industrialized it is! As I walk along the ridges, the view to the north and east is one of warehouses, factories, ports, and refineries. Lines of boxcars and tankcars move along on tracks like dutiful beasts of burden. In a water treatment plant below, huge tanks of water are swirled and purified. Trucks and cars move along freeways. Cylindrical oil tanks appear to climb the nearby hills like tract developments.

When I look west and south a totally different view greets me. The Bay is like a great inland sea—a Mediterranean—with various cities and islands visible around it. On this summer Sunday, there are already hundreds of sailboats out on the waters.

I look down below at the green lawn I have just left, and to my amazement I find that I am stunned by its beauty. From a distance it looks like a wondrous island, tropical and jewel-like in its greenness, with pines instead of coconut palms waving in the breezes. People have arrived now for their Sunday picnics, and I watch tiny figures playing on the lawn. One of these figures—from this great distance I cannot tell whether it is a boy or a girl—wears a white shirt and red shorts, and is chasing a frisbee across the lawn with long-legged strides. This person strikes me as utterly beautiful and I am momentarily shaken by a feeling of intense longing.

I return to the picnic areas and lawns, willing to look at them afresh. The crowd is mixed—blacks, Hispanics, and whites in about equal numbers. The sizzle and smell of barbecues rises up from various braziers. Families are playing ball on the lawns—wonderfully casual games where flattened soda cans serve as bases and grandma is cheered wildly as she hits a not-so-sharp single to left field. In a quiet corner of the park a man is sitting crosslegged on the grass, playing jazz on a flute. A white egret is poised on the edge of the lagoon. People are clustered around picnic tables, and I simply cannot get out of my head the notion that they are like the butterflies clustered around the wild buckwheat flowers on the hillside above.

Directions: Take Highway 80 (the East Shore Freeway) to Albany and exit at the Hoffman Blvd./San Rafael Bridge off ramp. Follow Hoffman to Cutting Blvd. Keep straight on Cutting (do not follow the flow of traffic when it turns right at Canal Blvd.) into Point Richmond. At the end of Cutting turn left on Garrard Blvd. and head through the tunnel. The parking areas for Miller/Knox are on the right.

Point Isabel

On September 15, 1888, according to an old newspaper account, a group of picnickers got into their horse-drawn carriages and headed north from Oakland, "slowly wending through green marshes and along the sandy beach to a picturesque peninsula known as Point Isabel.

"Under spreading buckeyes upon a brink overlooking the Bay, a pit had been dug and walled with flagstones in which a roaring fire was kept up until the sides were red with heat. The embers were then removed and into the pit sacks of clams and mussels gathered from adjacent tidelands were emptied.

"Over this was spread a species of seaweed, colloquially termed rockweed, and upon this was strewn corn and potatoes, over which another layer of weed was placed, pans of genuine Boston baked beans were laid, after which, the pit was filled with rockweed and covered with sacks to prevent the escape of steam."

Needless to say, a hundred years have brought dramatic changes to the art of picnicking, and to that "picturesque peninsula known as Point Isabel" as well. The Point lies off Hoffman Boulevard, just to the north of Golden Gate Fields, in an industrial area of Richmond. Instead of buckeyes, warehouses are now scattered over the peninsula. These warehouses, most of them dogmatically rectangular, would seem huge in another context. But here they are dwarfed by a leviathan of a building, the blue-and-white U.S. Bulk Mail Center—one of twenty-one such gigantic centers around the country built to handle second, third, and fourth class mail. The Bulk Mail Center and most of the other warehouses are in one unfortunate sense quite remarkable: despite the fact that they might have commanded sweeping views of the Bay, many of them were built almost entirely without windows, as if to express their total indifference toward this environment.

It is in such unpromising circumstances that we find Point Isabel Regional Shoreline, a thin strip of land about 300 feet wide that forms an L along the western and northern edges of the peninsula. It has a paved path about a half mile long, turfed areas, a few picnic tables, and an active parking lot.

The people who tend to visit Point Isabel are not the typical backpackers, swimmers, or campers you might find in other, more remote, East Bay Regional Parks. A salesman in a late-model Oldsmobile, for example, pulls into the parking area and, away from the eyes of his employer, stares out at the water for a few minutes before nodding off to sleep. A half hour later he wakes up and drives away without ever having gotten out of his car. Three men in a public utilities truck arrive, pull out lunch bags and thermos bottles, and take a leisurely coffee break at one of the picnic tables. Dog owners bring Rover and Fido for a midday romp along the asphalt path; Point Isabel is so popular with dog owners that they have even formed an association, PIDO—Point Isabel Dog Owners. Two lovers arrive in separate vehicles, and for the next hour or so walk slowly, hand in hand, along the bayshore. People come here for a variety of practical reasons—to meet a friend, walk the dog, take a break, or catch a nap. But something more basic is drawing them, too: namely, I believe, a deep-rooted human desire to go to the edge of the land and gaze out upon the sea. It is an impulse (or is it a need?) that is elemental, irresistible, as soothing as a deep breath, and seemingly as universal. At any given time throughout the world, there are thousands upon thousands of people standing at land's edge, on wharves and beaches, under palm trees and next to ice floes, gazing out at the sea.

I, too, come to Point Isabel on occasion to look at the water, and also at the birds. It is late fall, and a change of weather and glance at the sky tell me that the fall and

winter migrations of water birds are underway. Tens of thousands of geese and ducks are pouring down the Pacific Flyway from their summer nesting grounds in Alaska and Canada. At least a few of them, I reason, will be offshore at Point Isabel. And because the Point is in direct line with the Golden Gate, there is always the possibility of seeing some rare (for the Bay) ocean birds such as kittiwakes, shearwaters, and pelagic cormorants.

I walk along the asphalt path, taking note of the ingenious landscaping: the earth on the landward side has been banked into a small, continuous, undulating ridge so that the warehouses to the east are blocked from sight, and one's attention is focused on the spectacular view of the Bay to the west. I settle into the rocks along the shore and take out binoculars and a field guide. People walking their dogs nod at me in an indulgent and neighborly way, and I nod back.

It has been nearly a year since I have seen many of these birds, and I renew my acquaintance by glancing at their "nametags"—those strong patterns and colors that serve as identification: the two-toned black and white of the lesser scaups, the perfectly circular and perfectly white cheek patches of the goldeneyes, the white necklace and bushy head of the red-breasted mergansers, the large bill and snow-capped forehead of the surf scoters. I watch a double-breasted cormorant take off, so heavy and thick in flight that I am not sure it will ever quite lift off the water. I settle into the rocks, losing all thought of the asphalt path and the warehouses behind me, enjoying the calm attentiveness that comes from naming and observing, savoring the minor pleasures of birdwatching, when something happens that is quite unexpected and hardly minor.

The sun, which has been setting quietly in the west, suddenly collides with the horizon and bursts apart, spilling waves of color, flooding the sky with layers of pink, salmon, and peach. The colors swell in intensity. They pour into the waters of the Bay and wash over the mountains on the Marin shore. A cloud bursts into flame, as if by spontaneous combustion. I lower my eyes for a moment. The mud flats around the peninsula are saturated with a deep, grayish pink. An egret, standing humpbacked in a pool of glowing water, glances up at me; its eyes—burning like tiny embers—are startling reminders that even today extraordinary beauty can still be found on that "picturesque peninsula known as Point Isabel."

Directions: Take Highway 80 (the East Shore Freeway) to Richmond and exit at Central Ave. Follow Central Ave. west to the bayshore and the entrance to Point Isabel.

Point Pinole

"You've never been to Point Pinole?" my friend Dave once asked, looking at me as if I was some sort of cretin. "You've been to Paris, but you've never been to Point Pinole? Go! Right now! You simply can't live another day without seeing Point Pinole."

I did get to Point Pinole (the first time was in 1971). I jumped the fence and evaded the guard hired by Bethlehem Steel who then owned the property. I felt totally bewildered—like Alice must have felt when she slipped down the rabbit hole into a new world. Here, in Richmond, California, one of the most highly developed industrial areas of the world, I found: three-and-a-half miles of nearly virgin shoreline; over one square mile of rolling meadows; rare saltwater marshes with almost extinct birds; spectacular views across the Bay to Mount Tamalpais and the Marin coast; and, most welcome of all, a sense of spaciousness, depth, and tranquility rarely found anywhere else in the Bay. Visiting Point Pinole was like stepping into a mirage.

It still is like stepping into a mirage, except today you no longer have to jump the fence or play hide-and-seek with the Bethlehem Steel guards. Thanks to the urging of conservation groups, the East Bay Regional Park District has bought Point Pinole, and the 2,000-acre Point is now ours!

In the springtime the spacious meadows come alive with greens, flowers, brooks, and meadow creatures. I once came upon what I thought was an invasion of grasshoppers; it turned out to be toads, millions of tiny colorful toads, hopping crazily over the meadows like dust motes in the sun.

Another time, I was staring at a flower when to my amazement I saw a gallery of owls' heads staring back at me from among the petals. I had come upon owl's clover, one of the most plentiful wildflowers which grow on Point Pinole. And everywhere on the Point are groves of weeping eucalyptus trees, housing some of the biggest, most impressive hawks in the Bay Area.

Point Pinole is a good place to watch shore birds. If you want to get in on the action, come in the morning at low tide. (During the afternoon the setting sun creates a glare on the Bay that makes birdwatching difficult.) You will probably see more birds than you ever thought existed.

If you are a beginning birdwatcher, you may find the following guide somewhat helpful:

• If the bird is sitting on a piling, sunning itself and looking wise, it is probably a cormorant.

• If the bird looks too delicate, like a tissue paper origami creation, it's probably a heron or an egret.

• If the bird looks like a duck and it dives deep for its food, it's probably a canvas-back, grebe, loon, or scaup.

• If the bird is a duck and paddles around the shallows dipping for its food, it's probably a mallard, scoter, teal, or pintail.

• If the bird is wandering over the shore intensely studying the ground as if it lost something important in the mud, it's probably a sandpiper, avocet, stilt, or marbled godwit.

• If the bird flushes out of the pickleweed-cordgrass swamp, look sharp! You may have chanced upon an extremely rare California clapper rail or a salt marsh song sparrow.

You can watch birds, have picnics, fish, fly kites, or do almost anything you want at Point Pinole, but most people end up just wandering around. You can follow the shoreline for miles, alongside grassy meadows that roll gently down to the beach, or under sea bluffs that tower fifty feet above your head. This shoreline collects some of the most fascinating litter in the Bay Area. Pieces of wood, metal, fixtures, plastic spoons, and other familiar objects of civili-

zation emerge from the Bay warped, corroded, encrusted with barnacles, and invaded by seaweed. An ordinary tin can becomes transformed by the Bay into a grotesque piece of sculpture.

Along with manmade objects you also find seashells, crabs, seaweed, the body of a shark, or the delicate skeleton head of a heron. This flotsam is like the leftovers of a rich man's banquet: only a hint of the wealth of the Bay and a welcome sign that despite all we have done, the Bay is still very much alive.

People who come to Point Pinole usually leave with a feeling of peacefulness, and a few unanswered questions. What are the peculiar bumps, humps, dips, and pits that are scattered throughout the meadows? What was the long pier near the tip of the Point—recently reconstructed as a fishing pier—originally used for? Why did this land stay so unspoiled, right in the middle of Richmond? How did it escape the fate that befell almost every other piece of bayshore land in the East Bay?

Since the Civil War, Point Pinole has been used for the manufacture of gun powder. In the late 1890s Giant Powder Company (later Atlas Powder Company) began making dynamite and then nitroglycerine here. To guard against the "big bang," the manufacturing process was not carried on all under one roof as in ordinary factories, but in dozens of little buildings half-buried in the ground and spread out over a huge area.

The precautions were extraordinary. There were several full-time safety specialists, and their word was law. Employees were searched at the gate to make sure they carried no matches. They could wear no metal, not even belt buckles or nails in their shoes, since metal might strike a spark. A narrow-gauge train that ran between the buildings was powered by batteries. The pushcart that actually entered the buildings ran on hardwood rails rather than metal rails. Each day only as many explosives were manufactured as were needed to fill immediate orders. They were packed into aluminum crates. The crates were dipped into paraffin to seal them tight and were then brought to the pier. At the end of the day barges took the entire day's production out to waiting ships, and Point Pinole closed down for the night.

For about a hundred years a high fence and tight security kept the general public out of Point Pinole. As an accidental by-product, automobiles, factories, supermarkets, and housing developments were also kept out.

"Why choose the most beautiful place in the whole Bay for a munitions factory?" I used to wonder. I wondered about that for a long time, in fact, until one day the truth dawned on me. In the mid-nineteenth century the whole bayshore was as open and beautiful as Point Pinole. Point Pinole is different from downtown Oakland, downtown San Leandro, or downtown Richmond in only one respect: because of its curious history it has been left pretty much alone.

The explosives industry boomed (so to speak) until 1947, when a freakish accident in the Gulf of Mexico signalled the end. A shipload of ammonium nitrate fertilizer exploded, wiping out Texas City, Texas, killing or injuring over three thousand people, and rattling buildings 160 miles away. If cheap fertilizer packed such a wallop, reasoned many people, why use expensive nitroglycerine? And over the next decade ammonium nitrate came to replace the more traditional explosives.

In the early 1960s Atlas Powder Company closed down its Point Pinole operations and sold the land to Bethlehem Steel. Bethlehem planned to use this vast acreage to build the world's largest steel mill and export steel to the Far East. But by the late 1960s Japan had developed a strong steel industry of its own, and Bethlehem Steel no longer needed the land it had purchased.

For the next several years the destiny of Point Pinole hung in the air. Many Richmond officials wanted the Point industrialized or subdivided—"to keep it on the tax rolls." But conservationists launched an impressive and passionate *Save Point Pinole* campaign. Finally, in 1972, Bethlehem Steel agreed to sell Point Pinole to the East Bay Regional Park District. Today Point Pinole is in the domain of picnickers, beachcombers, and weekend fishermen who have been bringing in excellent catches of flounder, sturgeon, and striped bass from the fishing pier and from its shoreline.

With the return of fishing the history of Point Pinole has come full circle. The Huchiun Indians, one of the Ohlone tribal groups, had a permanent encampment in what is now San Pablo, and they too used to visit the Point frequently to fish. Then in 1772 Pedro Fages led a small company of soldiers into the area. The Europeans were tired and hungry, and the local Huchiuns brought them a nourishing porridge made of acorn flour, seeds, and the grains of wild grasses. The Spaniards called this porridge *pinole,* after an Aztec word, and the grateful explorers gave this name to the whole area.

Today we are all explorers. Many of us are disillusioned and puzzled by the civilization we've created, and we too are setting out to find wild places. Point Pinole is one of the best of these wild places, and I think that it will be as hospitable to you as it was to the Spanish explorers almost exactly two centuries ago.

Directions: Take Highway 80 (the East Shore Freeway) to Richmond and exit at Hilltop Dr. Follow Hilltop west to San Pablo Ave. Turn right on San Pablo, then left onto Atlas Rd. When Atlas Rd. meets Giant Highway, turn left to the park entrance.

San Leandro Bay

San Leandro Bay Regional Shoreline lies between the Oakland Airport and the Nimitz Freeway. It includes over 1,200 acres of saltwater marshes, mudflats, bay water, and solid land, yet nowhere in this expanse are you ever isolated from the industrial sights and sounds of East Oakland. A distant view might include objects like the Oakland Coliseum, a two hundred foot tall gas tank, or hillsides scarred by quarrying. The sounds you hear are those of Boeing 747s landing and taking off, trucks changing gear, locomotives bumping boxcars into order, motor boats whining, helicopters beating the air, and the hummings, buzzings, and knockings from dozens of factories that rim the park. From one of these factories come loudspeaker messages such as: "Mr. Smith, a call on line five. Mr. Smith, line five."

When I visit San Leandro Bay Regional Shoreline, I am well aware of the industrial setting (you can't help it), but—as if tuned to two channels at the same time—I am much aware of the natural setting as well. I am sitting in a canoe, drifting toward a piece of isolated marshland, my attention totally absorbed by a great blue heron that must be at least four feet tall. As I drift closer, it stands unutterably still. A momentary breeze tosses sequins over the water and ruffles the bird's feathers ever so slightly. Then the air falls still again. Small sandpipers scurry about beneath the heron. I am so close now that I can see the lavender tones on its neck. At last the heron lifts off. In the most liquid of motions it draws its neck in toward its body, straightens its legs out behind it, and slowly, sensuously strokes the air with its wings.

The loudspeaker repeats the announcement: "Mr. Smith, a call on line five. Mr. Smith."

The heron describes a long, easy arc as it heads toward another part of the marsh.

"Hey, Smitty," I think to myself. "Tell whoever is on the phone that the check is in the mail or the widgets have been sent Federal Express, get out of the office, and see what this place has to offer."

San Leandro Bay Regional Shoreline lies within a short distance of thousands upon thousands of Smitties, and it offers an unexpected, thoroughly unique, natural experience in and around the fringes of this industrial hinterland. There are usual and unusual "amenities," such as a small beach for sunbathing, picnic tables, an observation platform for marsh watching, a ramp for launching boats, several all-weather trails, acres of lawns, and a bathtub regatta every August to keep you laughing the rest of the year. There are also some seventy acres of saltwater marshland that turn deep russet every autumn and harbor a rich animal life, plus shorebirds without number that collect here, especially in the fall and winter.

My two favorite activities at San Leandro Bay are boating and birdwatching. I tend to take my canoe out when the tide is high and I can paddle around the sheltered bay right up to the margins of Arrowhead Marsh. For those with more ambition—and bigger boats—there are buoys that mark the channel into deeper bay water.

Birding is possible any time, but it is best when the tide is ebbing. As the water draws away from the land, it exposes extensive mud flats upon which thousands of sandpipers, dowitchers, avocets, willets, and other shore birds skitter. They are all studiously poking and probing into the mud. The littlest birds with the littlest bills eat from the uppermost layers of the mud; medium-sized birds with medium-sized bills eat further down; those with the longest bills probe the deepest.

Thousands of birds eat here day after day, year after year. What can they all be eating, you wonder. How can mud produce so much food?

From a human perspective, mud is certainly one of the

least exciting and least attractive things in the world, and certainly one of the most maligned. You can't build on it easily, walk or drive across it very well, and it gets all over you. Yet from the perspective of a worm or a mollusk, mud is an environment luxurious beyond reckoning. Tons of it are brought into the Bay each day from rivers and run-off in the form of suspended silt. As long as these billions of individual particles of silt are carried by fresh water, they retain a slight surface charge that makes them mutually repulsive, so that they stay dispersed in the water. As soon as this silt reaches salt water, however, the surface charge is reversed and the individual particles attract one another (I'll bet you didn't know they had it in them!). They now become mutually cohesive, pulling together and sinking to the bottom. As they settle, these billons of little particles don't quite key into one another, so that they are a loose assemblage with incredible surface area, holding vast amounts of oxygen, algae, and microscopic animal life. This provides an ideal environment for roundworms (nematodes), ribbon worms (nemerteans), and segmented worms (annelids) as well as small crustaceans and a number of mollusks such as mussels, clams, and snails.

To understand this environment better, wander down to the shoreline sometime and push your finger into the mud. It is fresh-smelling and wholesome, unexpectedly frothy and porous. It is not quite liquid and not entirely solid, but something in between.

At one time the entire San Leandro Bay area was "something in between"—not quite land, not quite water. Saltwater marshes extended inland past the present site of the Oakland Coliseum, where they met the freshwater marshes formed by the many streams that emptied into San Leandro Bay: San Leandro Creek, Elmhurst Creek, Arroyo Viejo, Lion Creek, East Creek, and Peralta Creek. Indeed a hundred-and-fifty years ago the margins of the Bay were indeterminate, without clear boundary between land and sea. This was the landscape that nurtured the Indian people who lived along the shores of the Bay for thousands of years, and fostered the great abundance of fish and bird life—the great flocks of birds that were said to darken the sky during migrating season.

But our current civilization hates indeterminate states and unclear boundaries; it prefers straight lines and sharp distinctions. Since the middle of the last century some areas have been filled with earth to create solid land, and the various creeks have all been culverted and channelized so that the land would not be flooded. Other areas were dredged to create deeper channels for boats. As a result the marshland of San Leandro Bay, which as late as 1915 comprised about two thousand acres, was reduced to seven-hundred acres by 1960. By 1972, only seventy acres of marsh remained.

Considering what this area was like a hundred-and-fifty years ago, San Leandro Bay has been severely degraded. Try viewing it, however, from the perspective of a mere fifteen years ago, when this was a forlorn and forgotten piece of wasteland on the fringes of a burgeoning industrial area. If it was visited at all, it was by caravans of garbage trucks which dumped piles of trash to create a forty foot high hill known locally as Mount Trashmore. This was land doomed to neglect and ruination. If the pacing of development had been any faster, the entire area might have been filled, dredged, and engineered to industrial ends with scarcely a voice raised in protest.

The restoration of San Leandro Bay is a mark of the extraordinary change in our attitude toward nature that has occurred in the last fifteen years. There is, of course, no way that we can restore this land to what it was like a century-and-a-half ago; there is no magic wand that will make the Oakland Airport and the Nimitz Freeway disappear. The development of a park at San Leandro Bay, however, does offer hope that we will once again let nature into the inner recesses of our cities, that we can live and work in better harmony with the birds, plants, and wildlife, and that nature will not necessarily be something far away—protected and off-limits, to be visited only on weekends—but that it can be mixed with factories, airports, freeways, and our homes, to be enjoyed on a daily basis.

Before disappearing from sight, the heron issues a low, hoarse call, haunting and strangely beautiful—a call that I hope Mr. Smith and all the other Mr. Smiths and Ms. Smiths will be hearing more and more as the years pass.

Directions: From Highway 880 (the Nimitz Freeway) exit at Hegenberger Rd. in Oakland. Go west on Hegenberger. Sections of the park can be reached by taking either a right onto Edgewater Dr., or further along on Hegenberger Rd., a left onto Doolittle Dr.

LAKES

There were once twenty-one creeks that flowed like bright silver ribbons from the Oakland-Berkeley Hills down into the Bay. Engineers, with the complicity of the city, county, state, and national "officials," have stolen almost all of them. They have channelized, boxed, dammed, and culverted them out of existence. They stole them away so cleverly that today most of us city folks would never guess that a few blocks from our houses once ran a living creek.

But as we are coming to realize, this was a melancholy theft. Years ago, when the thievery was still in the planning stage, we should have listened more lovingly to the babble of our creeks instead of the babble of engineers. We'd be happier people if tree-lined creeks still flowed past our homes and meandered in and out of our daily thoughts. I might say to my neighbor (after commenting on the weather): "The water level is dropping in the creek, the neighborhood swimming holes will soon dry up, and the buckeyes will lose their leaves." These creeks were like lifelines that connected our cities to the hills, the rains, and the rhythms of nature. When engineers stole the lifelines they left us even more stranded and cut off than we were before.

The creeks no longer flow through our cities—at least not as living creeks—but the waters have not disappeared. The waters are waiting for us in the hills as artificial lakes, big calm bodies of water standing patiently behind their dams, willing to give comfort to anyone who comes looking.

Some of my friends have a kind of snobbishness toward these lakes, as if they owed it to the environment to hate artificial lakes. These lakes are all too recent, they feel. None of them existed in the days of the Indians or even the Spanish. They don't belong. They're newcomers, intruders, usurpers of the landscape.

But except for a handful of Ohlone and Miwok descendants, we're all newcomers, intruders, and usurpers. The environment would be in much better shape if we all moved out. But we won't, and neither will the lakes. We cannot redo the past. But if we look honestly and openly at the present, we notice that the lakes which we have built are far from ugly. What we witness instead is an exciting interchange between a misguided technology that destroys creeks to build lakes and a patient nature which is clothing these lakes with beauty.

Building a lake, for all its ambiguity, has got to be one of the best pieces of magic in the world. It beats anything Houdini has ever done. Take a dry piece of land, wave the magic bulldozer, add lots of water, and stand back. Boom! Reeds, rushes, sedges, willows, tules, and dozens of other water plants burst out of the ground as if they had always been there, waiting for the day the waters would arrive. Ducks splash down upon the lake and nest in the cattails. Turtles and frogs materialize out of thin air and immediately go about their ancient business. Fish jump out from the depths to snap at water bugs, while the shoreline becomes riddled with the dens of foxes, raccoons, and other animals who prosper near the new lake.

A new lake may look half-finished for a few years. But after a short time an artificial lake is no longer "artificial"—at least not to the plants, animals, and birds who inhabit it. Older lakes like Temescal and Chabot which were built a century ago have nestled so comfortably into their landscapes that they look almost as much at home in the East Bay as an oak forest.

The East Bay Regional Park District manages lakes throughout Alameda and Contra Costa counties. A cluster of them, the Alameda Creek Quarries in Fremont, are currently used only by fishermen and await further development. Jewel Lake, in Tilden, is set aside as a bird refuge. The other lakes (Anza, Chabot, Contra Loma, Cull Canyon, Del Valle, Don Castro, Shadow Cliffs, and Temescal) offer fishing, hiking, boating, and—except for Chabot—swimming.

For up-to-date information on swimming hours and on fishing and boating regulations, call the East Bay Regional Park District at 531–9300.

Alameda Creek Quarries

Surely there is no stranger park in the Bay Area than the 459-acre Alameda Creek Quarries Regional Park, a group of twelve flooded gravel pits clustered around Alameda Creek, near the town of Niles. The scene of what was once a brutal, open-pit mining operation, much of the land remains gouged and scarred, the earth scraped bare in places, with deep holes and eroding cliffs. Other parts of the quarry land are thickly vegetated with the oddest assemblage of plants I have ever seen—walnut trees, almond trees, weeping willows, prickly pear cactus, tobacco bush, and shrubs and trees so exotic that I can't begin to identify them. If you were to lead me blindfolded into this jumbled landscape, then remove the blindfold and ask me where I was, I might guess Utah, Nevada, or even Central Asia— not Fremont, California.

It is no mere geological accident that deep gravel beds are found in this particular place, for it is here, at the edge of the alluvial plains, that Alameda Creek changes character. Throughout the rest of its 700-square mile watershed, the waters of the creek roil downhill, in their haste tearing rock from the hillsides and sweeping it along, grinding, crushing, rolling, and polishing it. At the site of Alameda Quarries the waters emerge from the Niles Canyon and enter the flat plains of Fremont. Here the water abruptly slows, nearly stops in fact, and as it does so its capacities change dramatically. This change can be expressed in a simple, elegant mathematics. When a creek slows to one-half its previous speed, the quantity of rock it can carry is reduced thirty-two times; the size of a rock that can be transported by pushing or rolling is reduced sixty-four times. Thus when the creek reaches the mouth of Niles Canyon and becomes suddenly languid, it drops almost all the rock it has been carrying—just as it has been doing for millions of years. In fact, the deposits of gravel in what geologists call "The Niles Cone" are now some four-hundred feet deep. The earliest quarrying was a "backyard" operation that hardly scratched the surface. James Shinn, who settled here in the 1850s and established an exotic plant nursery, would regularly dig gravel out of the creek bed every summer. The winter's floods were enough to fill the shallow holes with the next year's supply.

By the 1890s, however, the Central Pacific Railroad was removing thousands of tons of gravel from the area. Activity increased and an aerial photograph taken in 1939 shows gravel pits extending well beyond the creek bed. And by the 1950s, Kaiser, Rhodes-Jamieson, and other industrial giants maintained massive quarrying operations. From dawn to dusk the air was filled with what sounded like a continual avalanche, as gravel was dug out of the earth, crushed and sorted, and transported by truck or train from the area.

As the quarries were dug deeper—some of them are seventy feet deep—they filled with water, and as years passed increasing quantities of water had to be pumped out. But the continual pumping of water was expensive, and it also created an environmental crisis. The Fremont area derives most of its water from wells dug into the ground, and as the water was pumped out of the quarries it drained the water table. Farms in western Fremont were also pumping huge quantities of water out of the ground at the same time for irrigation, and by 1967 the groundwater level had dropped to sixty-seven feet below the surface. As a result, salt water from the Bay began to seep into the aquifers and threaten the entire southern Alameda County water system.

It was clearly necessary to raise the water table, and in the late 1960s and early 1970s the Alameda County Water District took a number of measures. It installed pumps near the Bay to help keep the salt water out. It limited groundwater withdrawals by agriculture and industry. And it purchased the quarries, now being abandoned by industry, and put them to use as percolation ponds. To do so the Water District built two inflatable dams across Alameda Creek next to the quarries. These dams lie limply across the creek, looking vaguely like the carcasses of beached whales, and they are watched twenty-four hours a day by guards lest some vandal shoot a hole in them. But

the dams nevertheless do their job. They impound the creek water which is then pumped into the quarries, and from the quarries it percolates back into the ground, thus replenishing the water table.

Today the quarries are very much "managed": by the Alameda County Water District for water production, by the East Bay Regional Park District for recreation. This is, then, an area with powerful institutional connections— friends in high places, as it were. Yet when you visit the park, there is very little sense of "institution" at all, except for a landscaped picnic area, a couple of outhouses, a few fences, and a scattering of "no trespassing" and "no swimming" signs. Indeed, the overall impression you get is that rather than being regulated and controlled, this strange landscape is more like a "badlands," a lawless-looking, abandoned land outside the fringes of civilization. Terns dart through the air like large, white swallows, now and then plunging into the ponds to catch fish. A flock of ducks forge through the water toward the setting sun, creating a number of silver V's, each with a duck at its apex. It is all a little jarring—the deep peacefulness of standing water placed within a gouged, mangled, yet undeniably exciting landscape.

Alameda Creek Quarries is not yet fully developed as a recreation area. Swimming is strictly forbidden, and most of the ponds are still fenced off. A few people come to Shinn Pond to fish for bluegill, bass, catfish, and blackfish. A model boat club meets regularly for races at "Kaiser A" Pond. And there is the opportunity—not to be missed—to walk around in this strange world.

Plans are currently being drawn up for a full-scale recreation area. They will have to be most unusual plans, for the question here is not the ordinary one—how to preserve a natural resource. The land is too severely altered for that. Nor can these scarred "badlands" be prettified with tame lawns, picnic sites, and a cute swimming lagoon without enormous (and utterly misguided) effort. I don't know whether it's possible, but my personal hope is that with such a haunting landscape, such bizarre plants, and such a strange history, the park planners will see this area for what I think it is—an artistic challenge—and they will create out of it a bold, dramatic recreation area unlike any other in the Bay Area.

Directions: From Highway 880 at Union City, take the Alvarado-Niles (east) exit. Go approximately five miles along Alvarado-Niles Rd. and its continuation, Niles Blvd., to "H" St., just before the town of Niles. Turn right on "H" St. to the Niles Community Park. Park here and take Alameda Creek Trail a couple of hundred yards to Shinn Pond.

Lake Anza

Lake Anza is a small, nine-acre lake located in Tilden Regional Park. It offers swimming—and with its cattails, rocky outcroppings, nearby forests, and mountainous landscape, it is one of the most picturesque lakes in the Bay Area. I know it, now you know it, but unfortunately we're not alone. Hundreds of thousands of other people know about Lake Anza. And they all seem to show up on hot weekends when you are likely to find "No Admittance, Beach Full" signs posted at the entrance. So be forewarned.

Fishing is also permitted here, but apparently no one has yet told the fish (if there happen to be any).

The lake was created in 1939 by damming a portion of Wildcat Creek. Its original purpose was to provide water for the lawns and greens of the new Tilden golf course. It was named after Captain Juan Bautista de Anza, the great colonizer of the Southwest, who along with José Joaquin Moraga led an expedition through this area in 1776.

Lake Anza is one of the best of the Park District's walk-around lakes. The entire hike takes only twenty minutes or so, but it leads you through some truly fine scenery and involves you in a few minor adventures: treading across the dam, mountain goating on top of some rocks, crossing Wildcat Creek, and mucking your way through a willow swamp. And there are many side excursions you can take. You can sit out on the rocks that protrude into the lake, posing perhaps like that winged sylph in the old White Rock ads. You can wander out over the meadows. Or you can follow the rushing waters of Wildcat Creek through a dark, rocky canyon of oak, bay, and a few redwoods.

Or if your body seems to be mated to your beach blanket for the day, why not send your head on an exciting journey of its own? The sandy beach and grassy lawns are arranged like an amphitheater where everyone looks out across the lake at the spacious scenery of Tilden. If you sit back far enough on the lawn you can also look out over some extraordinary people—Berkeleyites who crowd the shores of the lake on hot days.

I've enjoyed myself at Lake Anza whenever I've gone, but my favorite times are in the early spring and late fall when, if it's a warm day and a life guard is available, the Park District will sometimes open Lake Anza for swimming. (Call 531–9300 to find out for sure.) On days like this, when the weather is balmy, the surrounding hills are still green, and there are only a scattering of people on the beach, Lake Anza (which is beautiful in any case) seems to achieve perfection.

Directions: From Highway 24 take the Fish Ranch Rd. exit just east of the Caldecott Tunnel. Follow Fish Ranch Rd. up hill to Grizzly Peak Blvd. and turn right. Turn right again at the South Gate entrance to Tilden Park, and descend into the canyon. At the Botanic Garden turn left onto Wildcat Canyon Rd. Keep bearing to the right. The entrance to Lake Anza is on the right, just before you reach the merry-go-round.
   See Map N.

Lake Chabot

Lake Chabot is a very peaceful lake. It is big (315 acres) and it feels big; yet because of an island in the middle and its many bays and inlets it seems at the same time intimate. People come to fish, hike, boat, or just sit quietly along the banks. The peacefulness of Lake Chabot is contagious. The only squabbling you are likely to hear is among the ducks and the geese.

Lake Chabot's profound calm gives almost no hint of its grotesque beginnings. The lake was built in 1874 by Anthony Chabot, a hydraulic engineer fresh from the gold country. His method of construction was revolutionary. He first aimed gigantic water hoses at nearby hills and washed thousands of tons of earth into San Leandro Creek. Then he imported herds of wild mustangs to gallop back and forth over the loose earth to compact it into a dam.

The water backed up slowly behind the dam, and by 1876 Lake Chabot was formed. Then nature took over. It revegetated the barren hills and lined the lakeshore with tules. Ducks, herons, and egrets came to nest. Grebes, loons, geese, and coots visited and stayed. Deer broke trails to the shore. Raccoons and foxes found dens along the banks. People created Lake Chabot, and nature accepted the creation.

But as far as East Bay residents were concerned, Lake Chabot was a hidden garden. It remained off-limits to the public for the next ninety years. Fishermen stared longingly over the fence. Rumors spread about five pound trout and nine pound bass, innocent, reckless fish prowling the lake, ready to chomp down on the first hook.

Even Water Company officials acknowledged that the major "fishing problem" at Lake Chabot was too many fish. This was especially true in the drought of 1918 when the water level dropped drastically. Fish moving through the shallow water stirred up silt which clogged the filters and stopped the flow of water into Oakland. That year imaginative Water Company personnel introduced sea lions into the lake to eat the fish. But the sea lions had other ideas. Homesick, they were seen humping and thumping their way over the hills toward the Bay.

As the years passed the demand for public access to Lake Chabot grew stronger, and, in 1966, the Water Company gave in. The fence came down. On opening weekend an estimated 30,000 fishermen stampeded to the lake. And, wonder of wonders, those crazy rumors proved true. Some lucky folks actually did catch five pound trout and nine pound bass, and they still do. Today Lake Chabot is one of the best stocked of all the Park District's lakes, and it is one of the most popular fishing spots in the Bay Area.

The swimming is undoubtedly as good as the fishing, but only the ducks know for sure. Lake Chabot is officially classified as an emergency water supply. And (as you may remember from childhood trespasses) the Law is unbelievably uptight about people peeing in the water supply. Thus swimming is absolutely forbidden, an injunction, I'm sorry to report, that is strictly enforced by park personnel.

Although you can't swim here, the lake is good for boating. It is big enough to make boating an adventure, while its narrow fingers keep you in close contact with the surrounding landscape. There are no facilities for launching your own boat—it's forbidden—but you can rent a rowboat, pedal boat, canoe, or an electric motorboat. You can also try the excursion boat which circles the lake on summer weekends.

In addition to boating and fishing, I hope you'll also take a walk. One of my favorite hikes is along the eastern shore of the lake toward Honker Bay. The path is asphalted most of the way, which makes it very good for bikes, baby carriages, and trikes. The further you get from the Marina, the more quiet and pleasant the lake becomes. The vegetation is more varied, with especially fine stands of cream-

bush, cow parsnip, and that pungent smelling plant called mugwort from which absinthe was once made. You pass through some oak-bay woodland, scrub brush, and small meadows—while along the lake red-winged blackbirds, wavering like flags on cattail stalks, lecture you on the innumerable virtues of being a red-winged blackbird.

Once in the narrower parts of Honker Bay head across the footbridge. From the land of shade and coolness you enter the land of sunshine and heat. You've passed from a north-facing slope to an exposed south-facing (sun-facing) slope. The temperature is noticeably hotter here, and lizards scurry along the trails, apparently stimulated by the heat. Instead of trees and shrubs with broad soft leaves, you find a grassy hillside splotched with stiff coyote brush, and topped by a forest of wispy eucalyptus. At this point you can walk a bit further around the lake, until you reach the trail that climbs the slope to Chabot Family Camp; or you can continue until you have encircled the lake, a curiously satisfying experience.

I tend to take longer hikes when I go to Lake Chabot, but I suspect that, whatever anyone does here, they leave feeling very relaxed. Whether paddling a boat over placid waters, trying to catch a fish, hiking up a fern and oak canyon, lying down in a flowery meadow, or enjoying a family picnic, almost everyone at the end of the day seems to have absorbed some of the peacefulness and gentleness that radiates out of Lake Chabot.

Directions: From Highway 580 (east), exit onto Castro Valley Blvd., turn north onto Lake Chabot Rd., and follow it to the park entrance.
See Map D.

Contra Loma

Contra Loma is a small lake with a sandy beach, green lawns, and a cattail fringe. It is surrounded by seven hundred acres of grassland. Seen from the air during the summer it looks like a sparkling blue-green jewel set in the vast golden meadows outside Antioch. There's swimming, fishing, and a unique hiking experience.

The first time I visited Contra Loma I tramped around the lake searching for the creek that feeds into it. It was a charming walk. Mallards, canvas-backs, coots, and a heron had staked out various parts of the lake. A delegation of Canadian geese followed after me, strutting around like a group of congressmen and bankers. My footsteps triggered off the splashing of frogs, while within the water scores of muskrats were diving, swimming, twisting, playing, disappearing and reappearing, obviously having a wonderful time. Yet as I checked out the topography, I didn't find any sizable creek that might have created this lake. And (as one might deduce from the dry, nearly treeless hills) there's not much rain here either. It was all very perplexing: where could this water have come from, I wondered. And then I met a fisherman.

"Catch anything?" I asked, and he showed me a flounder.

So now I had two mysteries: where did the water come from, and what in the world was an ocean fish doing flopping around in a freshwater lake?

Contra Loma (as I later found out) was built in the late 1960s by the U.S. Bureau of Reclamation as a storage reservoir for the Contra Costa Canal System. The water for this system is pumped out of the San Joaquin River at Rock Slough, and it is carried by a network of aqueducts throughout eastern Contra Costa County. The water is used for industrial, agricultural, and domestic services. At one point pumps draw the water out of the canals and force it up through underground pipes into Contra Loma Lake. Here the water sits, waiting patiently in the bullpen, so to speak. If at any time the pumps at Rock Slough have to be shut down for repairs, water will be drawn from Contra Loma to keep the canals operating.

Now that we know where the water comes from we can solve the mystery of the misplaced flounder. Saltwater fish, flounders have made their way from the Bay into the Delta and up the San Joaquin River, where the fry (small enough to pass through the screens) get drawn through the pumps and are dashed and tumbled into the canal system. They swim along the canals until eventually a few get sucked in by a second pump and are deposited in Contra Loma Lake.

Once the flounder fry reach Contra Loma they undertake another, far more astounding journey—a journey that every member of the flounder family must go through. In their infancy flounder fry are almost indistinguishable from any other small fish. They are symmetrically shaped, a bit like a torpedo, with no hint whatsoever of their future appearance. They hatch from eggs that float upon the surface, and for their first month or so they stay near the surface, feeding on minute organisms. But at the age of about four weeks, when they are no more than a half-inch long, they desert the surface, sink to the bottom, and lie down on their sides. Then begins a remarkable transformation. The skull twists and distorts until the lower eye (which is staring unproductively at the mud) "migrates" around the top of the head to the up-facing side of the fish. The body flattens out, the lower (eyeless) side turns white, the upper side turns a darker color, and the fins undergo further changes until (how incredible it must be to experience this!) a flounder is created.

Some people visit Contra Loma to fish—striped bass (a saltwater fish) and black bass (a freshwater fish) are caught.

But during the summer most visitors are here to swim. The lake sits in a bowl which collects heat and keeps out the brunt of the wind. On marginal beach days, when it seems a bit chilly in Oakland, you might remember that it's probably just right at Contra Loma.

The land surrounding Contra Loma is predominantly meadowland, some seven hundred acres of grass with only a couple of dozen buckeyes and blue oaks scattered over the slopes. During the last century grizzly bears, mountain lions, pronghorn antelopes, and elk roamed these hills. Captain Kimball, a pioneer resident of nearby Antioch, noted that on the morning of his arrival in 1849 he saw eighty elk in one herd. And much of the meat sold in local markets in 1850–51 was dried elk meat.

Today, of course, the big game is gone, and the land seems much emptier without them. The engineers and park planners who recently arrived to build Contra Loma Lake looked over the undulating golden-brown grasslands and they saw—well, to be blunt, they saw nothing! Their early reports kept referring to "barren grasslands," and the problem the planners faced was how to make these "barren grasslands" attractive to potential park users. "Plant trees," came the answer. Over five thousand trees were planted in 1969: Monterey pines, Coulter pines, Bishop pines, live oaks, sycamores, white alders, black walnuts, Arizona and Modesto ashes, Fremont poplars, moraine honey-locusts. . . . But no sooner were the trees planted than an amazing thing happened. Hordes of rabbits and mice rose out of nowhere and nibbled almost every one of the trees down to the ground. It makes you think. Barren?

To begin with, there are lots of rabbits, mice, moles, gophers, and ground squirrels at Contra Loma. Then there are all the animals that feed off them: gopher snakes, king snakes, rattlesnakes, foxes, badgers, hawks, and vultures. On hot summer days when *you* are most likely to be visiting Contra Loma, the wildlife is most likely to be hiding. But even the briefest walk through the grasslands will turn up dozens of burrows, scats, nibbled grass, and other signs of the rich wildlife that inhabits the grassland.

Despite its proximity to the Bay, Contra Loma is really part of the hot interior grassland environment. In the spring the grass is green and cool, rippling in the wind, flecked with exquisite wildflowers. Everybody loves to hike across the California grasslands in the spring.

But in the heat of summer there is a different sort of experience that is reserved only for the most hardy hikers. Climb to the top of a ridge and look over the big, billowing hills beyond Contra Loma's "bowl." The ground beneath your feet seems to be breathing with heat waves. You sweat, and sweat, and sweat, and the sun looms big in your consciousness. Ever wonder why many ancient people worshipped the sun? Contra Loma is an especially good place to find out. In the winter the sun is shy and kindly, in the spring gently insistent and nurturing. But almost every day during the summer the sun shows all its power. At first it may seem as if the sun is angry. Don't fight it, don't try to hide from it. Lie down in the meadow and submit. Let yourself be as passive as a piece of iron in the hands of a blacksmith. Let the sun beat down on you, pound against you, and melt you down into the smells of the meadow until it seems you no longer exist.

From this encounter with the sun you return feeling purified, cleansed, reborn, and perhaps a bit wobbly. Walk down the hill again and jump into the cool waters of Contra Loma Lake for what will undoubtedly be the most refreshing swim you have ever had anywhere.

Directions: From Highway 4, turn south at the Lone Tree Way exit in Antioch. Turn right (west) at Frederickson Lane, which leads to the park entrance.

Contra Loma is open for swimming throughout the year.
See Map B.

Cull Canyon

Cull Canyon in Castro Valley is a small 360-acre park with a lake. The main attraction here is swimming.

Like nearby Don Castro, Cull Canyon Lake was the creation of the Alameda County Flood Control and Water Conservation District. Whatever engineering virtues the lake may have, as a swimming hole it is impossible. The water level drops by as much as fifteen feet every year, leaving a broad ribbon of mud all around the shore. To provide for swimming a second dam was built on a side ravine that feeds into the lake. The area behind the dam was graded, and water was pumped from the lake to make a small, neat swimming area. Thus there are really two lakes here: the larger lower lake with its ducks, occasional fishermen, and fluctuating water level; and the small upper lake with its tidy beach, bath-house, redwood decks, sand, green lawns, and highly landscaped appearance.

While you are at Cull Canyon you might notice the nearly pure grassy slopes that rise above the lake. Elsewhere in the area, ungrazed meadowland is being encroached upon by brush. But here you'll find very little brush. Why are these slopes different from other slopes in the area? The answer is *fire*. Every few years accidental fires burn off brush seedlings and leave the hillsides blackened for the rest of the summer. When the fall rains come, seeds in the soil germinate and reclothe the slopes with almost pure stands of oats and a scattering of poppies and vetch. Such meadows are a good environment for deer and other big game. The Indians of California used to ignite their grasslands regularly to burn away the brush and create meadows much like this.

Most people who come to Cull Canyon don't think very much about Cull Creek, which feeds into the lake. In fact they may even be contemptuous of it. They know Cull Creek only from what they see near the tennis courts across Heyer Avenue from the lake—a small trickle of water dwarfed by a dam, a spillway, and an enormous sculpturesque concrete channel installed by the county Roads Division.

To visit the real, unimproved Cull Creek, drive upstream from the park further into Cull Canyon. This is one of the loveliest canyons in the Bay Area. S.W. Cull was a pioneer resident, and I imagine that the canyon is pretty much as he left it. Here and there stands a bulky, rickety, old-fashioned barn or stable, a trim wooden corral fence, and a horse whisking away a fly in the lazy sun. Cull Creek turns out to be a gentle little creek that flows peacefully between its tree-lined banks. The slopes above the creek are a charming mosaic of cow-dotted meadows and thick oak woodlands stretching leisurely over the hills.

The beach at Cull Canyon is a very pleasant place to spend the day swimming and sun-bathing—which is exactly what most people do. But what makes Cull Canyon Park particularly interesting to me is the bird life here. The mixture of meadow, forest, brushland, streamside, and lake provides a varied environment that attracts a large number of birds. There are so many birds at Cull Canyon, and they're doing such interesting things, I hope on your next visit you'll check them out.

How do you watch birds? You might, of course, make a big production out of it. You bring binoculars, field guides, boots, a pencil, a notebook, a checklist, and a dozen bird whistles. With a look of dour determination on your face you go stomping into the brush and do you know what? At the end of the day you'll be stung, blistered, scratched, tired, and nasty—and all the birds will have fled into the hills, scared out of their little wits.

Then again, you might be more casual about it. Bird watching can be a lazy person's sport. While you're fishing, sun-bathing, or lying under a tree, you listen carefully and look. Be quiet, peaceful, alert, and you'll begin to see birds everywhere. You'll see long-legged birds wading on stilts along the stream; web-footed birds paddling across the lake; plump birds rustling in the leaves; tiny birds buzzing like bees at flowers; hunters and scavengers patrolling the sky; birds with yellow feathers, blue feathers, gold, red, orange, or green feathers; birds gulping insects, stabbing fish, cracking seeds, sipping nectar; birds chasing each other madly through the trees without ever once crashing into the branches. Look around and you'll be amazed at what fantastic things you'll see.

Or forget about looking, close your eyes and listen to the bird songs that fill the air: songs that pierce, twitter, and cascade; songs like bright ribbons spread over the sky; songs tossed down as freely as confetti. I used to imagine that the birds were singing out of joy and sexiness. Now bird scientists tell us that much of the singing is to stake out a territory and warn away intruders. I'm delighted to learn this. What a marvelous way to settle territorial battles. Imagine if every time a person I didn't like came to my door, instead of being rude or grouchy, I could chase him away with a song. What songs I would learn to sing! It makes me envy the birds all the more. I envy them their flight, I envy them their ingenious way of settling disputes, and I envy them the privilege of spending each warm summer day around the lake at Cull Canyon.

Directions: From Oakland, take Highway 580 south and follow it east toward Stockton. After Castro Valley, take the Crow Canyon exit. Follow Crow Canyon Rd. to Cull Canyon Rd. and the park entrance.

Del Valle

Del Valle is a huge 3,800-acre park with a lake five miles long. It is located in the hills above Livermore, and it has swimming, boating, wind-surfing, fishing, camping (see page 193), and hiking.

It was along one of the trails here that I once spent the morning watching a bird gather materials for its nest. The bird flew from the brush to a nearby meadow and plucked out a piece of straw. But it did not rush right back to its nesting site. Instead it flew with the straw to the top of a bush. There it paused for a long time, rocking in the wind, balancing itself with the straw like a tightrope walker with a balancing pole. And it sang a song. The song was a torrent of clear sound, continuing so long and so loud that I was amazed that such a drab bird could possibly contain so much of it. I half expected the bird to collapse like a deflated balloon from its efforts. But at the end of the song the bird looked just as plump and fresh as before. It hopped to the top of another bush and again surveyed the landscape. Finally, after several more bushes and another aria or two, it plunged into the thickest part of the brush and disappeared. A few minutes later it emerged again to fetch another piece of straw. The whole process was very leisurely. An efficiency expert would have been appalled at the unnecessary flourishes and wasted motions. "Now this is the proper way to build a nest," I can hear the efficiency expert lecturing. But when you visit Del Valle, listen to the birds within you, not to the crew of efficiency experts we all carry within us. I hope that you'll spend your day here wastefully and creatively—with the same unhurried and alert exuberance as a bird building its nest.

Del Valle is one of the best places you can go to quiet a noisy mind or relax a restless body. It is big enough to absorb you easily. In fact, the size of the lake puts Del Valle in a category of its own. While most of the other lakes in the East Bay are neighborhood swimming holes, Del Valle is more on the scale of a state or national recreation area. (In fact, officially it is a California State Recreation Area, managed by the East Bay Regional Park District.)

The lake has seventeen miles of shoreline. You can swim at the sandy beaches. You can bring a boat or rent one—a rowboat if you want to exercise your arms, a pedal boat if you want to exercise your legs, or a sailboat if you want to exercise your brain outmaneuvering the tricky little winds that (sometimes) come in from the surrounding hills. During the summer this long, narrow, placid lake is busy with the activities of thousands of swimmers, fishermen, and boaters. But in early fall most of this activity abruptly ends, as the lake goes through a drastic change.

To understand this change you have to know something about the way the lake works. It was built in 1968 by the State of California primarily for recreation. Other reasons given were flood control and water conservation. The water that fills the lake comes from Arroyo del Valle Creek, but in dry years the State pumps extra water from the Delta to bring the lake up to recreational standards. And the State keeps the lake brim-full until about September 15th. By then the kids have returned to school and recreation demands decline. At the same time the South Bay counties are experiencing their seasonal water shortages. So the valves are opened, and the waters of Del Valle begin a southward journey. During the fall the water level in the lake drops by as much as eight inches a day.

Before the lake was built, there was a magnificent, broad valley here, shaded by immense sycamores, pines, and oaks. As I watch the water level drop, I keep hoping that this magnificent valley will reappear, intact and magical, like the lost city of Atlantis. But of course it doesn't. The valley is irretrievably lost, replaced by this serene and stately lake. The immense valley trees no longer shade cattle or hold nests of birds, but they still serve life-

sustaining functions. They lie at the bottom of the lake
where they provide homes and nutrients for the large fish
population of Del Valle. These trees, with the help of
heavy stocking, make this one of the best fishing
lakes in the Bay Area, with its large numbers of trout and
black bass. And all winter long, as the lake begins to swell
once more from the incoming waters of the creek, Del
Valle is left primarily to fishermen and to the few hikers
who continue to wander over the hills.

The land around Del Valle is different from other park
land in the East Bay. Elsewhere, we are accustomed to the
struggle between meadowland and forests. On dry sites
the grass wins out, on moist sites we find thick, condensed
forests. But at Del Valle the battle seems to be a draw.
Thriving broad meadows are dotted everywhere by trees.
The trees are not close enough together to form a true
forest and overshadow the grasses. So grass and trees live
together in peaceful co-existence, and the result is perhaps
the best of both environments. You can enjoy the shade,
character, and bird life of a forest while wandering through
open flowery meadows. Yellow-billed magpies strut
around like movie stars. Ground squirrels race into their

holes at the slightest provocation. Cows with dull, grumpy faces graze among the soft blades of grass.

In the winter and spring Del Valle has one of the most inviting environments I know, beckoning you to leave the trails and roads and wander aimlessly along the lakeshore, into the cool canyons, and high up into the billowing hills. During the summer, however, the sun bakes down upon the valley. The hiking season now ends as people gather around the shores of the lake to swim and keep cool.

During the hottest days of summer you might look up at the surrounding hills and wonder how the various plants survive. Why don't they just wither and die? Every plant you see at Del Valle has had to solve the problem of summer heat, and some of their solutions are ingenious.

Sycamores and willows handle the problem quite simply. They grow near creeks with their roots perpetually in water. As the sun draws moisture out of their flat broad leaves, more moisture is drawn up from the groundwater below.

Plants like the digger pine and chemise have solved the heat problem by reducing their leaves to thin needles. The less leaf surface there is, the less water evaporates.

Other plants—like live oak, coyote bush, and manzanita—have developed thick leaves coated with a waxy substance, cutin, which protects the inner cells from the intense heat.

The leaves of black sage are covered by a tiny forest of hairs. At night these fuzzy hairs trap moist air next to the leaf's surface, and they maintain this friendly microclimate during most of the next day.

Then there is the buckeye tree, which is deciduous. But instead of dropping its leaves during the fall like other deciduous trees, the buckeye loses its leaves during the heat of summer. It conserves water by going completely dormant in the hottest months.

Annual wildflowers handle the summer heat by trustingly dying each spring. Only the seeds lay on the hot earth all summer, closed up tight against the beating of the sun. In the fall the first rains come, but the seeds don't respond.

They are waiting for moisture plus warming soil, and this combination acts upon them like a trigger. Sometime in February the trigger goes off, and bang! Del Valle is transformed. Hiking now takes on a new excitement. Throughout the green grass there are explosions and the sparks fly. Wild fireworks spread over the ground. Flowers pour out over the meadows and flow right down to the borders of the lake. It is during this season that I want to pull people away from their TV sets, kidnap them if necessary, and get them out to Del Valle. The ground is covered with lilies, poppies, baby blue-eyes, shooting stars, Chinese houses, paintbrushes—dozens of different species of wildflowers. Some are soft, open, and utterly passive, like beds of silk sheets. Others are sharply defined, full of secrets and complexity. I love their soft living colors, their textures, and their fragrances. I have even come to love the thick silence that flowers surround themselves with. But my love is unrequited. It is not for me (or for you) that these flowers put on their annual show, but for the bees who will probe and twist within their silent wombs to complete the act of reproduction. Each flower strains to be as beautiful as it can to capture, seduce, for a few seconds enslave a bee that will complete its cycle. There are spring days at Del Valle when I too would willingly be enslaved, but it is our destiny to stand outside this sensuous world that scarcely acknowledges our existence—to stand outside it like strangers at a wedding, and to wonder at its almost excruciating beauty.

Directions: From Oakland, take Highway 580 east to Livermore. Exit at the North Livermore Ave. off ramp. Head south through town. North Livermore Ave. becomes South Livermore Ave., and eventually veers east to become Tesla Rd. From Tesla Rd., turn right onto Mines Rd. After about three miles turn right again onto Del Valle Rd. and the park entrance.
    Swimming is allowed at Del Valle throughout the year.
    See Map F.

Don Castro

Don Castro is not a Caribbean revolutionary, a Havana cigar, or a Puerto Rican rum. Even more exotic than these (the truth is indeed stranger than fiction!) Don Castro is an artificial lake in Hayward—a lake that has fish, turtles, ducks, and frogs as well as a separate swimming area with a clean beach, green lawns, and picnic tables. It was named after Guillermo Castro, a Spanish settler whose immense 27,000-acre land grant included what is now Hayward and Castro Valley.

Don Castro Lake was created in 1964 when the Alameda County Flood Control and Water Conservation District put a dam on San Lorenzo Creek. The water backed up behind the dam, and in a few years cattails, ducks, fish, and fishermen arrived to complete the lake environment.

In building the dam engineers needed thousands of tons of earth. They got it by flattening a nearby hill, and in the middle of the flat spot they dug a crater. When the lake had formed they pumped water from the lake into the crater and thus created a separate pool—the "swimming lagoon" as it's called. White sand was poured around the swimming area, a three-and-a-half acre lawn was planted,

and picnic tables, barbecue pits, a bath house, and shade trees were installed. In 1969 Don Castro was opened for swimming and picnicking.

The engineering history of Don Castro explains why there are two distinct environments here: a fairly natural lake environment for fishermen, hikers, and bird-watchers; plus a developed, carefully planned recreation area for swimmers, picnickers, and sun-bathers.

The swimming area is very pleasant and open. It has a roped-off space for little kids so they don't get in your way very much—and you don't get in theirs. Swimming is best here on weekends when there is hardly any truck noise on the nearby freeway.

The area around Don Castro has been a favorite recreation spot for many hundreds of years. Near where the dam now stands Indians used to have a sweathouse. Later, Chinese gamblers took over the spot and opened up a casino featuring fan-tan, faro, and the other slick gambling games of the last century. Today the East Bay Regional Park District offers swimming, hiking, and fishing. From Indians to Chinese gamblers to us, recreation has gone through some stunning changes. I sometimes wonder what the next century will bring to Don Castro. More inconceivable changes? Or have our culture and our tastes settled into a groove for a dynasty or two?

While most people come to Don Castro primarily to swim, I can never resist a hike around the lake. It takes no more than a half hour—an hour if you poke around—and is especially delightful if you have a kid or two tagging along. As you walk along the edge of the lake, there are many things to be aware of: dragonflies putting on shows of precision darts and dashes, turtles sunning themselves on half-submerged logs, frogs practicing their ventriloquist acts, and the nostalgic hummings and buzzings of a summer afternoon.

There is nothing really dramatic here, nothing very exciting. Just the scruffy, varied goings-on of a typical piece of left-alone California land. The most intensely moving thing I ever saw here was the battle—not between a mountain lion and a deer—but between a garter snake and a mouse. The snake had chomped down on the mouse, but was having trouble swallowing it. The mouse was too fat, the snake a mere adolescent. The snake tried and tried, maneuvering the mouse's body around until its head was aimed right down the snake's throat. At that point the squeaking and wiggling stopped. The mouse went limp, apparently dead. The snake paused and resumed its struggle, stretching its jaws to outlandish sizes trying to encompass the mouse's body. I watched fascinated. There was something horrible yet vaguely comic about this struggle. The snake rested and tried again. It kept at it for about a half hour. But the mouse was simply too fat. The snake finally gave up, backed off very quickly, and slithered away like a disappointed suitor without even a backward glance. A few seconds later the dead mouse stirred itself, staggered to its feet, wiggled its nose, and ran off into the bushes as if nothing out of the ordinary had happened.

If your love of nature is not satisfied by anything less than grandeur, a walk around Don Castro will seem silly. But if you want to look in on the lives of snakes, mice, dragonflies, hummingbirds, frogs, turtles, ducks, and whatever else you may see; if you have the patience to watch these ordinary animals go about their daily affairs, and if you have the humility to think deeply about their lives; then the walk around Don Castro is one of the best short hikes I know. Grander hikes leave me with the feeling of having been someplace special. The walk around Don Castro leaves me with the feeling of wanting to return again and again.

Directions: From Oakland, take Highway 580 south, then east toward Stockton. After Castro Valley take the Crow Canyon Rd. exit. Turn right immediately after exiting onto Center Street, then left onto Kelley St. (the second light) to Woodroe Ave. Turn left onto Woodroe Ave. which leads to the park.

Shadow Cliffs

Shadow Cliffs—well, to be perfectly honest about it, Shadow Cliffs is a hole in the ground. A 250-acre hole. It lies between Pleasanton and Livermore and has swimming, a sandy beach, excellent fishing, some boating, and a water-slide that has made it one of the most popular lakes in the East Bay.

The Sand and Gravel Division of Kaiser Industries began digging the hole in 1930 as a quarry. When they were through digging, they shut off the pumps and the deepest part of the hole filled with water. Now, if *you* were into big business, what would *you* do with a played out, flooded quarry? Obviously you'd try to give it away. In 1969 Kaiser presented this derelict quarry to the East Bay Regional Park District as a "gift." They valued the gift at $250,000—thus obtaining a tax write-off. The Park District then used this established land value to get $250,000 in "matching funds" from the U.S. Bureau of Outdoor Recreation, and with the federal money they went to work. They built a sandy beach, lawns, picnic area, ball field, and parking lot to create what Park District literature has called "a compact, sparkling recreation area."

Swimming is the most popular activity at Shadow Cliffs, and the water that filters into the lake through the surrounding gravel soil is deliciously clear and cool. There are also boat rentals and fishing. Black bass, red-eared sunfish, white catfish, and blue-gills have been planted in the lake, while carp have mysteriously sneaked in on their own. The lake is periodically stocked with rainbow trout. What in the world do all these fish find to eat in a place as sterile as an old quarry? Look along the south shore of the lake and you'll see some recently flooded brush and trees protruding from the water. These dead branches are the basis of a lot of the fish life here. Algae clings to them, and small forage fish and black bass fry find food and protection among the tangles.

Another place where the fish feed, breed, and hatch is just north of the beach area where you'll notice a grove of bushes extending into the water. These bushes look like willows, but they're not. They go by the curious name of mule fat. Unlike willows, which have long "catkins," these bushes have full, complicated little flowers and puffball seeds that tell you they are members of the Composite family—close relatives of sunflowers, asters and dandelions. I'm not sure why this plant is called mule fat. The best guess I've heard is that mules, which aren't nearly as fussy as horses, browse the bush enthusiastically.

Just over the levees from Shadow Cliffs is a section of Arroyo del Valle Creek that you might look at. This is a big, broad, green, slow-moving creek lined with willows and alders—a creek that to my eyes has more exciting and creative recreation possibilities than any developed area in the East Bay. And apparently the wildlife feel the same way. You would not ordinarily expect much wildlife in the vicinity of an old gravel pit, but the wildlife around Shadow Cliffs may surprise you. It surprised me. Part of the quarry above the water level has reverted to meadow and brush. I've seen ground squirrels, jack rabbits, raccoons, muskrats, deer, and many birds—some living here, others just passing through.

There's plenty of wildlife, fishing, and swimming at Shadow Cliffs. But beyond that there is something unique and even bizarre here. All around you at the horizon are the massive towers and conveyer belts of sand and gravel operations. On weekdays (and sometimes on weekends) you hear the noises of tons of rocks being sorted and poured, of huge equipment scraping and dumping, of boxcars crashing and clanging. It's a monstrous, fascinating, other-worldly scene of big machinery against a sharp blue sky.

The "cliffs" (which are really the sides of the original

gravel pit) are eroded, gray, full of shadows, lifeless, and bleak.

Lapping up against the cliffs is the water—cool, clear, peaceful, inviting. Ducks and coots paddle softly about. Fish splash and leave concentric circles. Delicate lacy trees line the water's edge. Everything is cool, clean, sparkling.

On the shore wildflowers are blooming, rabbits scurry in the bushes, and in the tall grass meadow-larks build their nests and raise their broods.

Shadow Cliffs is a combination of exquisite delicacy and mechanical brutality—as unintegrated, crazy, and surrealistic as the rest of American life. Except more so. Even if you don't swim or fish or care much about wildlife, maybe you ought to drop in on Shadow Cliffs anyway. For the artistic experience.

Directions: From Highway 580 take the Santa Rita Rd. exit south which becomes Main St. in the town of Pleasanton. Turn left onto Stanley Blvd. Follow Stanley Blvd. east to the park entrance.

The lake is open for swimming throughout the year.

Temescal

Temescal is a small, very pretty park. It has a lake, green lawns, secluded picnic areas, and a beach with white sand. Weeping willows lean out over the water as if to admire their own reflections. Butterflies flutter across the trimmed grass. Children hold out pieces of bread to white ducks that glide over the lake. Strollers set out on short hikes through redwood and pine groves. A few hundred feet away are two busy freeways and a power station—but these sights and sounds are mostly hidden from Temescal. People stretch out on the beach or on the grass—some clearly napping, some clearly awake, but most in a dream-like state somewhere in between.

An amazing thing about Lake Temescal is that most of this charming environment is man-made. The lake, of course, is artificial. The eucalyptus trees in the background come from Australia, the pines that shade the picnic areas are from the Monterey Peninsula, the weeping willows are natives of Eurasia, and even the redwood grove near the south parking lot is planted. The big stone building near the beach is the accounting office of the East Bay Regional Park District. Every sunny morning a park employee turns on the nearby miniature waterfall, and turns it off again before going home. The white ducks are domestic fowl gone wild. Very little is native at Temescal.

But if Temescal is so artificial, why in the world is it so pretty? Who was the genius who created this place? Was it Anthony Chabot who built the lake? Or the East Bay Regional Park District which runs it? Will the talented landscape architect in charge of this project please step forward and take a bow? But no one steps forward. The landscape architect, always present, forever modifying everything we do, is simply *Time*.

Lake Temescal is the oldest lake in the East Bay. It was created in 1868 by Anthony Chabot. He built it the way he later built Lake Chabot, by aiming water hoses at the surrounding land, washing tons of earth into the creek, and compacting the earth under the hooves of wild horses. Lake Temescal was originally meant to supply the tiny town of Oakland with water. But we all know what happened to the "tiny town of Oakland," and by the 1870s larger reservoirs had completely replaced Temescal. The lake was left alone to grow old and seasoned. Time chipped away at the sharp edges of artificiality, blended the diverse elements that were later added, erased what didn't belong, and shaped Temescal into the most natural-looking of all the artificial lakes.

Before Temescal was a lake it was, of course, a creek. Ohlone Indians had a village along its shores, and in the village they erected a communal sweathouse. They used the sweathouse to cleanse themselves (like a sauna), to cure illness, and in spiritual exercises. Before going on a hunt they bathed thoroughly to rid their bodies of human odors, and then they rubbed pungent herbs over their bodies to become even more like the vegetation around them. Franciscan missionaries named the creek "Temescal," a name derived from two Aztec words: *tema* (to bathe), and *cali* (a house).

To thousands of Oakland–Berkeley residents summertime means Lake Temescal. It is our backyard swimming pool, and the lake is very popular—especially on weekends. If you want to enjoy a little solitude, come on weekdays or at "off" hours.

If you don't care about swimming, but you are looking for an exceptionally lovely walk within minutes of the city, try Temescal on a foggy morning, when wisps of fog chase each other across the glass-like water, and when the lake with its backdrop of trees looks like a scene from a Chinese landscape painting. Or come during a light drizzle when the rain patters softly on the water, and the whole world seems painted in shades of gray. On such drizzly winter days your arrival is greeted by a delegation of geese who waddle out of the water—fierce-looking, honking geese, dancing heavily toward you like a line of overweight cheerleaders, whooping it up for the local river god who still presides over the happenings at Temescal.

Directions: Take Highway 24 to the Broadway exit in Oakland. Follow signs to Highway 13. The parking area is on the right side of the road before reaching Highway 13.

A smaller parking area to the south of the lake can be reached by taking the Broadway Terrace exit from Highway 13 (the Warren Freeway). Follow Broadway Terrace a very short distance west to the park entrance.

TRAILS

The East Bay Regional Park District has almost exactly one thousand miles of trails. Trails are cast over every regional park like a coarse net, and strands of the net go beyond the park boundaries to connect with other parks and with lands owned by other public agencies. Some trails are old ranch roads that loop easily over high, open ridges. Others are narrow footpaths scratched into the land, scarcely more sophisticated than deer trails. There are trails that plunge into redwood forests, parallel the course of streams, lead to the summits of peaks, follow the shoreline of the Bay, and encircle lakes. There are trails that lead you through chaparral, through freshwater marshes, or across open meadowland. Over the years I have walked virtually every inch of these trails, often several times, and I am continually amazed at how much beauty has been captured by this net of trails.

The two trails described in the following pages stand largely isolated from the other regional parks. Alameda Creek Trail follows the banks of Alameda Creek from the Bay toward the town of Niles, and the Lafayette–Moraga Trail follows the deserted right-of-way of an old railroad. These trails are both paved, and stretches of them pass through heavily-settled suburban areas. Probably too civilized to interest back-country hikers, they are nevertheless a joy for local bicyclists, joggers, people pushing baby strollers, for those looking for a place to walk after several days of winter rains, and for those open to the possibility that natural beauty can sometimes be most deeply felt where it is least expected.

Alameda Creek Trail

Alameda Creek Trail follows the banks of Alameda Creek from the mouth of Niles Canyon to the Bay—a 12-mile stretch that shows the effects of generations of flood control engineering. The creek's course has been straightened, its banks riprapped to the proper "angle of repose," and its waters regulated by upstream dams and drawn upon along its length for a variety of needs. Its flood plain—a huge area over which it once ranged freely—has been given over to suburban tract developments, farms, and factories.

Today Alameda Creek is very much under control— curbed, regulated, sadly obedient at all times. Yet not so long ago it was wild and magnificent. The largest creek in the East Bay, it was so pre-eminent in the minds of the early settlers that they named the county after it.

Alameda Creek originates high on the slopes of Mount Hamilton (elevation, 4,212 feet), and as it cascades toward the valleys below it is gradually augmented by Valpe Creek, Calaveras Creek, Arroyo Hondo, and San Antonio Creek. When it reaches Sunol Valley, it is fed by Arroyo de la Laguna, which itself draws water from Arroyo Mocho and Arroyo del Valle. Here, having amassed the flow from nearly seven hundred square miles of watershed, a powerful Alameda Creek bursts through the narrow Niles Canyon. At the mouth of the canyon, at the town of Niles, it emerges onto the plains of Fremont. Up to this point it is still reminiscent of John Muir's description of it almost exactly a century ago: "a sparkling stream which rises in the mountains and dances lightly along its rocky bed, singing softly to the hills and trees that line its course, cheerily greeting the little tributaries that join it at the mouths of deep ravines, now and then taking a wild plunge over a ledge of rocks only to recover its accustomed dignity the next moment—at length to spread out, clear and placid upon the breast of the Valley."

It is upon the plains of Fremont that drastic alterations have been made to Alameda Creek. Years ago it spread out so widely that today it is difficult to identify where its main channel might have been. In truth, on this broad alluvial plain it must, over the centuries, have been constantly filling old channels with silt and cutting new ones. The various channels thus cut would have been lined with huge cottonwoods, sycamores, and thick growths of willows, creating the shaded arcades that originally gave the creek its name. And the land between the various channels would have been swampy and subjected to repeated flooding during the winter months—home to tens of thousands of waterfowl that would have darkened the skies in their annual migration.

The long, indecisive, luxurious wanderings of Alameda Creek in its flood plain were brought to an end in the present century. To make the plains safe for farms and houses, the Army Corps of Engineers and the Alameda Flood Control District straightened the course of the river and confined its flow between strong walls of concrete from the mouth of Niles Canyon to the Bay.

It is alongside such a highly engineered environment that Alameda Creek Trail runs, following the banks of the creek for twelve miles from the town of Niles, through Alameda Creek Quarries Regional Park, through Fremont and Union City, past Coyote Hills Regional Park, and to the shores of the Bay. There are actually two trails here, one of gravel that runs along the northern bank, the other (more heavily used) of asphalt that runs along the southern bank. Whenever the trails meet a roadway they dip under it, so runners or bicyclists never have to break stride to wait for an automobile.

As an athletic facility, Alameda Creek Trail is a huge success. It attracts bicyclists and runners of varying degrees of proficiency. Some runners are local residents who slip out their back doors for a brief jog. Others, though, are of a different breed: serious, long-distance runners who have discovered that if they combine a round trip on this twelve-mile trail with a short loop around Coyote Hills Regional Park near the Bay, they have the exact distance needed for marathon training.

While athletically excellent, environmentally Alameda Creek is quite tame. This does not mean that it is lifeless. It isn't. There are small islands upon which ducks and geese still nest and raise their young. Terns diving into the water and egrets poised at the water's edge are proof of a decent fish population. Flocks of redwinged blackbirds are forever rising out of the reeds to show off their bright red epaulettes. I remember one day in particular when I found Alameda Creek Trail beautiful. It was in late January, and spring was arriving early. The buds on the willows had turned velvety and an acacia tree was in full bloom. The day was thick with fog, so thick that the air and the water in the creek were the same color, and could scarcely be differentiated. Seagulls cawed in the sky overhead, invisible in the fog. Occasionally one would swoop low enough to be seen, seeming to materialize out of the air, seeming to be made of exactly the same stuff as the air and water.

There are beauties to be appreciated along Alameda Creek Trail, and it makes for a good family bike ride between Coyote Hills Regional Park and the colorful town of Niles, which was, in the days before Hollywood, the movie capital of America. Alameda Creek Quarries Regional Park, near Niles, is well worth a few hours of exploration (see pages 144–147). What remains of the natural world of Alameda Creek, however, is a mere remnant, and it leaves people like me bemoaning the loss. Yet the past is gone—gone for good—so perhaps it would be wiser (and certainly more practical) to look to the

future. Today, with all the houses so recently built and the trail so freshly constructed, the area looks a bit raw. Yet someday perhaps the houses will nestle more comfortably into the landscape. Perhaps trees will be planted to shade the trail (which is now almost entirely exposed). Perhaps ivies or other plants will cover the bald concrete embankments. Perhaps the waterflow will be managed so as to encourage a richer riparian life along the creek. Perhaps someday Alameda Creek and the trail alongside it will attain elegance and beauty, like some of the old canals back east—an elegance and beauty that only age can give. I sincerely hope so. But I also hope that when future generations of people walk quietly in the shade of trees alongside the creek, they will still remember to tell tales of how utterly splendid and unspeakably lovely this creek was in the days of its youth.

Directions: The eastern end of Alameda Creek Trail can be reached from Highway 880 by taking the Alvarado-Niles Rd. (east) exit near Union City. Follow Alvarado-Niles Rd. and its continuation, Niles Blvd., about five miles to the town of Niles. Continue east on Niles Canyon Rd. (Rte. 84) just past Mission Blvd. to Old Canyon Rd. and a parking area.

The western end of Alameda Creek Trail can be reached from Coyote Hills Regional Park. (See page 220.)

Other convenient access points along its length include Newark Blvd., Hop Ranch Rd., Decoto Rd., and Jamieson Quarry on Paseo Padre Parkway, where these roads cross the Alameda Creek Flood Control Channel.

MAPS

Sharon G. Johnson

All trails shown in the following maps are open to hikers. People with special needs (equestrians, mountain bikers, handicapped, etc.), or those wishing up-to-the-minute trail information, should contact the East Bay Regional Park District at (415) 531-9300.

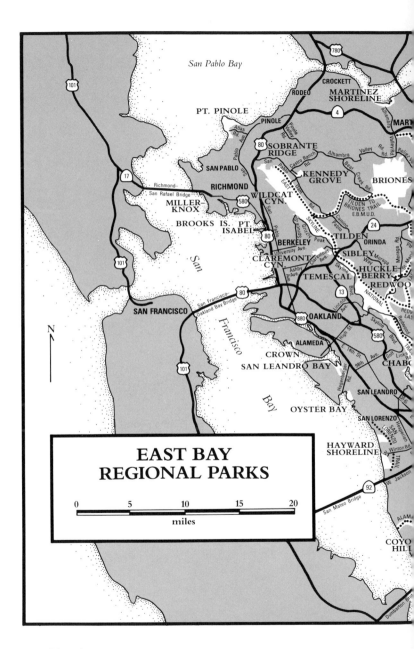

San Pablo Bay

780

CROCKETT

RODEO
MARTINEZ
SHORELINE

MART

PT. PINOLE
4

PINOLE

101
80
SOBRANTE
RIDGE

SAN PABLO
KENNEDY
GROVE
BRIONES

Richmond–
San Rafael Bridge
RICHMOND
580
WILDCAT
CYN.
TILDEN TO
BRIONES TRAIL
E.B.M.U.D.

17

MILLER–
KNOX

BROOKS IS. PT.
ISABEL
80
BERKELEY
TILDEN
24
ORINDA

SIBLEY

CLAREMONT
CYN.
HUCKLE-
BERRY
REDWOO

101
TEMESCAL
13
NATIONAL

San

80
San Francisco
Oakland Bay Bridge

SAN FRANCISCO
OAKLAND
880
580

ALAMEDA
CHABO

CROWN
SAN LEANDRO BAY

Francisco

101

SAN LEANDRO

OYSTER BAY
SAN LORENZO

Bay

HAYWARD
SHORELINE

92
San Mateo Bridge

ALAM

COYO
HILL

N

EAST BAY
REGIONAL PARKS

0   5   10   15   20

miles

Map A

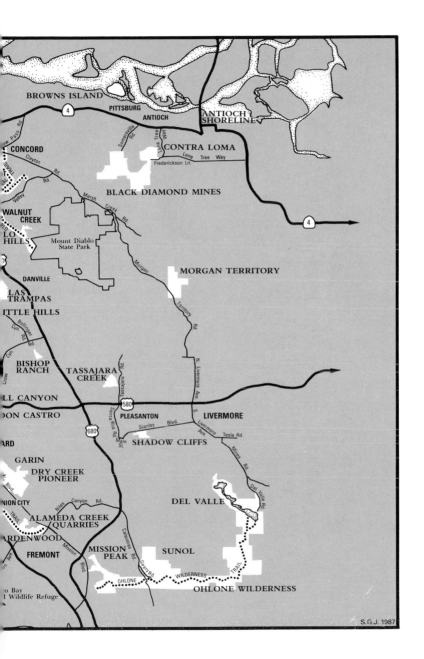

BROWNS ISLAND

PITTSBURG

4

ANTIOCH

ANTIOCH
SHORELINE

CONCORD

CONTRA LOMA

Lone Tree Way

Frederickson Ln.

BLACK DIAMOND MINES

4

WALNUT
CREEK

LO
HILLS

Mount Diablo
State Park

MORGAN TERRITORY

DANVILLE

LAS
TRAMPAS

ITTLE HILLS

BISHOP
RANCH

TASSAJARA
CREEK

LL CANYON

DON CASTRO

580

PLEASANTON

LIVERMORE

680

Stanley Blvd

ARD

SHADOW CLIFFS

Tesla Rd.

GARIN

DRY CREEK
PIONEER

NION CITY

Canyon Rd.

DEL VALLE

ALAMEDA CREEK
QUARRIES

ARDENWOOD

FREMONT

MISSION
PEAK

SUNOL

OHLONE

WILDERNESS

OHLONE WILDERNESS

o Bay
l Wildlife Refuge

S.G.J. 1987

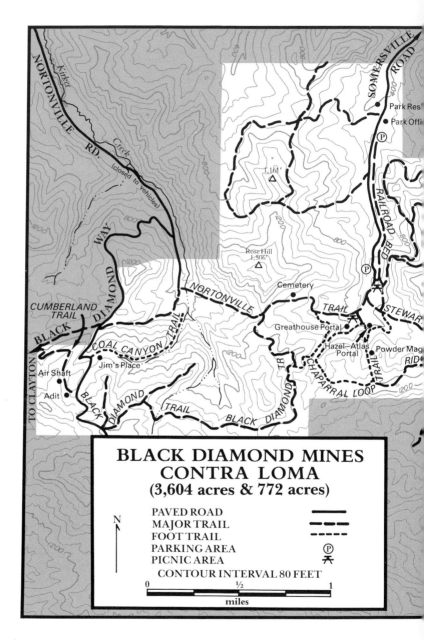

**BLACK DIAMOND MINES
CONTRA LOMA**
(3,604 acres & 772 acres)

PAVED ROAD	▬▬▬
MAJOR TRAIL	▬ ▬ ▬
FOOT TRAIL	▬ ▬ ▬ ▬
PARKING AREA	Ⓟ
PICNIC AREA	🎍

CONTOUR INTERVAL 80 FEET

0   ½   1

miles

Map B

IOCH AND PITTSBURG

Contra Loma Reservoir

CONTRA LOMA REGIONAL PARK

FREDERICKSON LANE

CONTRA LOMA TRAIL

RIDGE TRAIL

CORCORAN MINES TRAIL

TRAIL

MINER'S TRAIL

STEWARTVILLE TRAIL

Prospect Tunnel

STEWARTVILLE

STAR MINES TRAIL

Star Mine

LOOP CYN TRAIL

OIL CANYON LOOP TRAIL

OIL

S.G.J. 1987

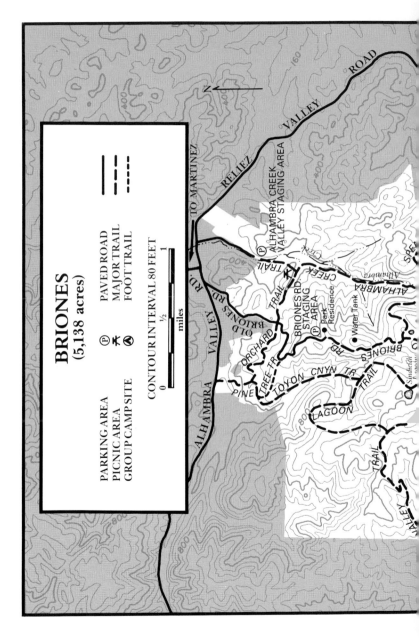

Map C

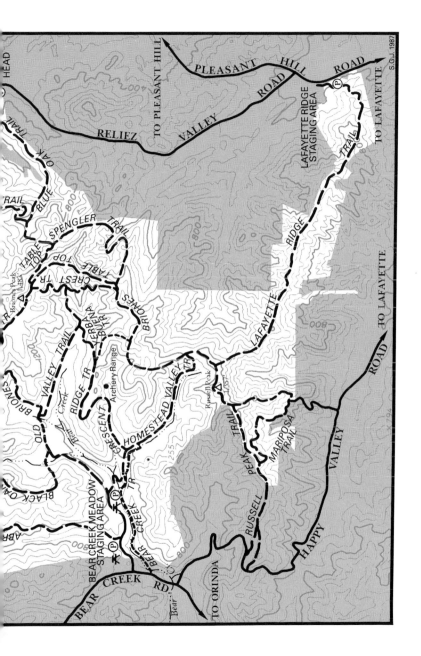

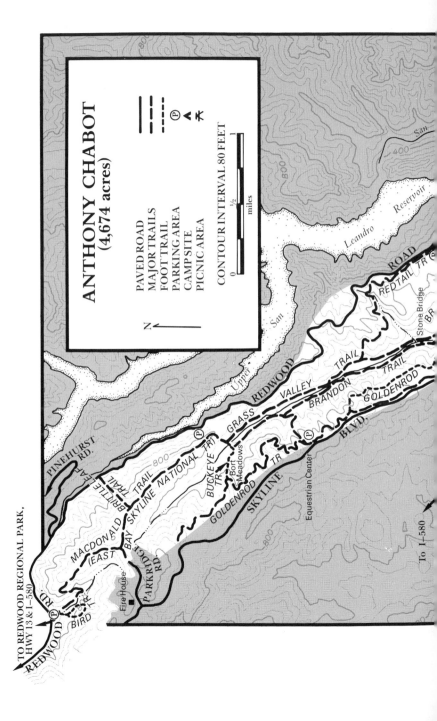

ANTHONY CHABOT
(4,674 acres)

PAVED ROAD
MAJOR TRAILS
FOOT TRAIL
ⓟ PARKING AREA
◣ CAMP SITE
⋔ PICNIC AREA

CONTOUR INTERVAL 80 FEET

0   ½   1
miles

N

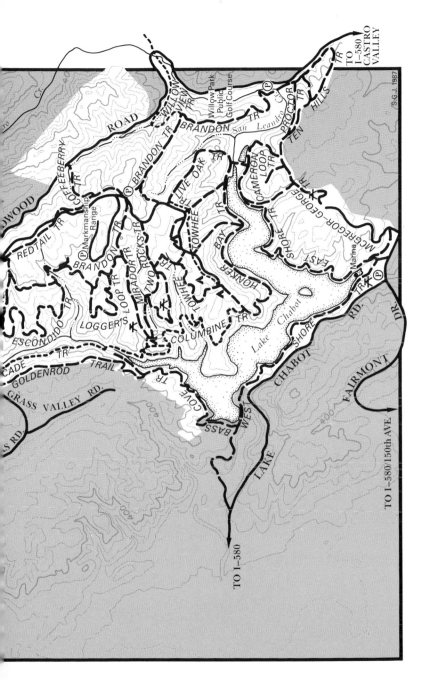

Map D

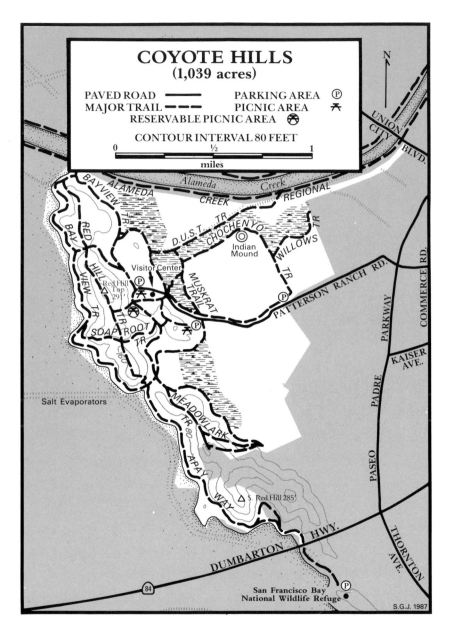

COYOTE HILLS
(1,039 acres)

PAVED ROAD —————   PARKING AREA Ⓟ
MAJOR TRAIL – – – –   PICNIC AREA ⚹
RESERVABLE PICNIC AREA ⊛

CONTOUR INTERVAL 80 FEET

0   ½   1

miles

N

UNION CITY BLVD.

Alameda Creek

ALAMEDA CREEK REGIONAL TR.

BAY VIEW TR.

BAY VIEW TR.

RED HILL VIEW TR.

D.U.S.T. TR.

CHOCHENYO TR.

WILLOWS TR.

Indian Mound

Visitor Center

Red Hill Top 291'

MUSKRAT TRAIL

PATTERSON RANCH RD.

SOAP ROOT TR.

COMMERCE RD.

KAISER AVE.

Salt Evaporators

MEADOWLARK TR. 80

APAY WAY

S. Red Hill 285'

PASEO PADRE PARKWAY

THORNTON AVE.

DUMBARTON HWY.

84

San Francisco Bay
National Wildlife Refuge

S.G.J. 1987

Map E

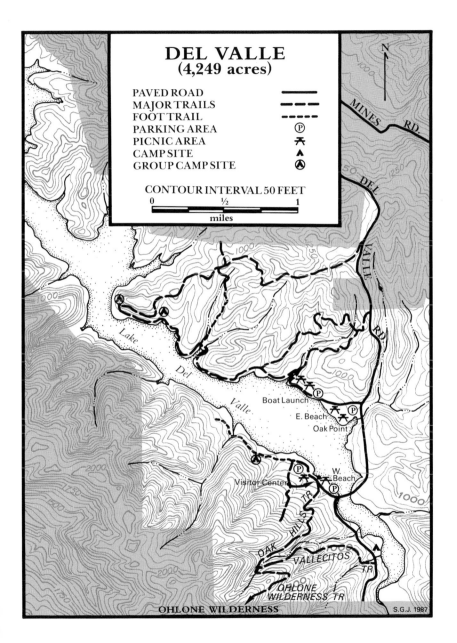

DEL VALLE
(4,249 acres)

PAVED ROAD	———
MAJOR TRAILS	– – –
FOOT TRAIL	- - - -
PARKING AREA	Ⓟ
PICNIC AREA	⚏
CAMP SITE	▲
GROUP CAMP SITE	Ⓐ

CONTOUR INTERVAL 50 FEET

0   ½   1
miles

N

MINES RD.

DEL VALLE RD.

Lake

Del

Valle

Boat Launch

E. Beach

Oak Point

W. Beach

Visitor Center

OAK HILLS TR.

VALLECITOS TR.

OHLONE WILDERNESS TR.

OHLONE WILDERNESS

S.G.J. 1987

Map F

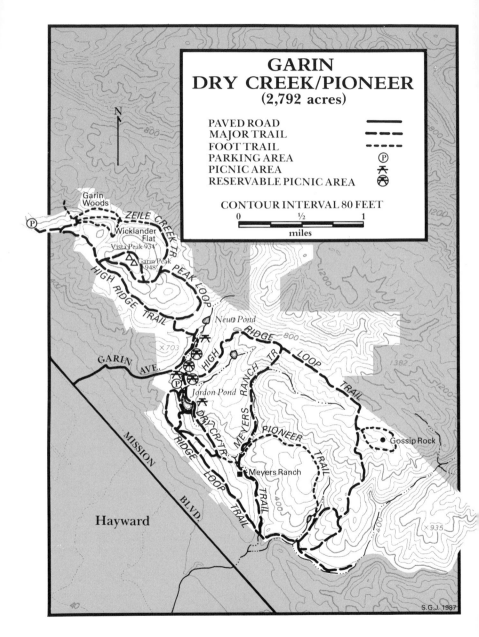

GARIN
DRY CREEK/PIONEER
(2,792 acres)

PAVED ROAD	————
MAJOR TRAIL	– – – –
FOOT TRAIL	- - - - -
PARKING AREA	℗
PICNIC AREA	⛢
RESERVABLE PICNIC AREA	◉

CONTOUR INTERVAL 80 FEET

0   ½   1
miles

Map G

S.G.J. 1987

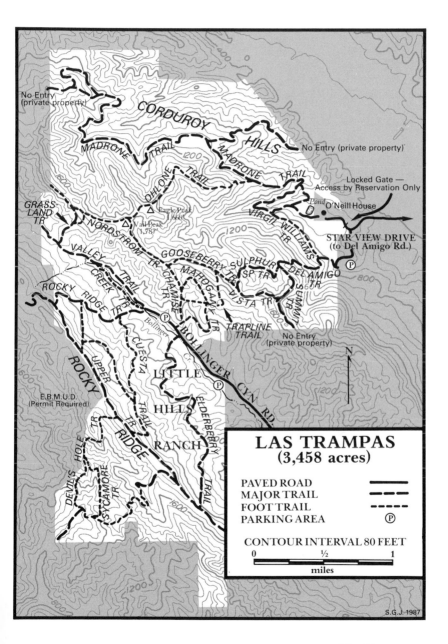

No Entry
(private property)

CORDUROY HILLS

MADRONE TRAIL

MADRONE TRAIL

OHLONE TRAIL

No Entry (private property)

Locked Gate —
Access by Reservation Only

Pond
O'Neill House

GRASS
LAND
TR

NORDSTROM TR

△ Eagle Peak
1,660'

△ Vail Peak
1,787'

VIRGIL WILLIAMS TR

STAR VIEW DRIVE
(to Del Amigo Rd.)

VALLEY TRAIL

GOOSEBERRY TR

SULPHUR
SP TR

DEL AMIGO
TR

CHAMISE TR

VISTA TR

SUMMIT TR

ROCKY RIDGE TR

CREEK TRAIL

MAHOGANY TR

Bollinger

TRAPLINE
TRAIL

No Entry
(private property)

N

ROCKY

UPPER

CUESTA TRAIL

BOLLINGER CYN RD.

LITTLE

HILLS

E.B.M.U.D.
(Permit Required)

RIDGE

RANCH

ELDERBERRY TRAIL

DEVILS HOLE TR

SYCAMORE TR

LAS TRAMPAS
(3,458 acres)

PAVED ROAD
MAJOR TRAIL
FOOT TRAIL
PARKING AREA ⓟ

CONTOUR INTERVAL 80 FEET

0   ½   1
miles

S.G.J. 1987

Map H

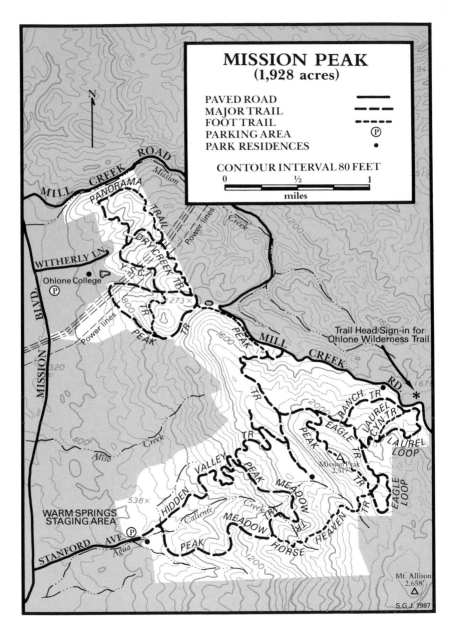

Map I

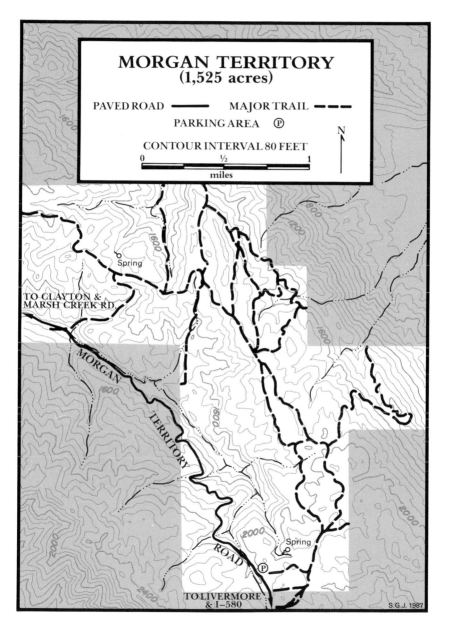

MORGAN TERRITORY
(1,525 acres)

PAVED ROAD ━━━━━ MAJOR TRAIL ━ ━ ━

PARKING AREA Ⓟ

CONTOUR INTERVAL 80 FEET

N

0   ½   1

miles

Spring

TO CLAYTON &
MARSH CREEK RD.

MORGAN

TERRITORY

ROAD

Spring

Ⓟ

TO LIVERMORE
& I-580

S.G.J. 1987

Map J

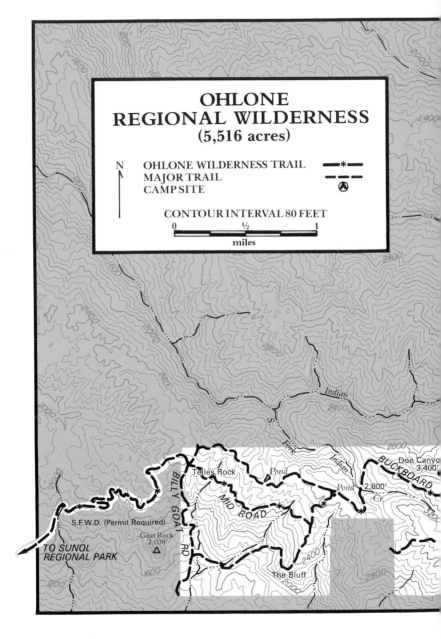

OHLONE
REGIONAL WILDERNESS
(5,516 acres)

N

OHLONE WILDERNESS TRAIL ———*———
MAJOR TRAIL — — — —
CAMP SITE

CONTOUR INTERVAL 80 FEET

0 ½ 1

miles

Indian

S. Fork

Indian

BUCKBOARD

Doe Canyon
3,400'

Telles Rock

Pond

Pond 2,800'

Cr

MID ROAD

BILLY GOAT RD

S.F.W.D. (Permit Required)

Goat Rock
2,038'
△

TO SUNOL
REGIONAL PARK

The Bluff

Map K

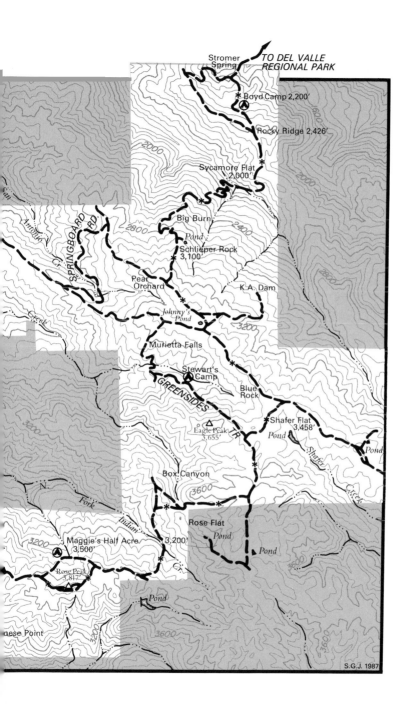

Stromer Spring

TO DEL VALLE REGIONAL PARK

Boyd Camp 2,200'

Rocky Ridge 2,426'

2000

Sycamore Flat 2,000'

Big Burn

SPRINGBOARD RD.

2800

Pond

Schlieper Rock 3,100'

2400

Pear Orchard

K.A. Dam

Johnny's Pond

3200

Murietta Falls

Stewart's Camp

GREENSIDES TR.

Blue Rock

Shafer Flat 3,458'

Eagle Peak 3,655'

Pond

Shafer Creek

Pond

Box Canyon

3600

3000

N. Fork

Indian

Rose Flat

Pond

Maggie's Half Acre 3,500'

3,200'

Pond

Pond

3200

Rose Peak 3,817'

Cr.

3600

Pond

aese Point

3200

3600

3600

S.G.J. 1987

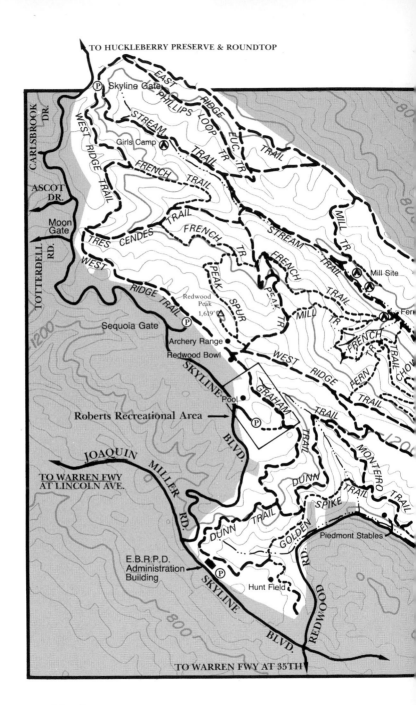

Map L

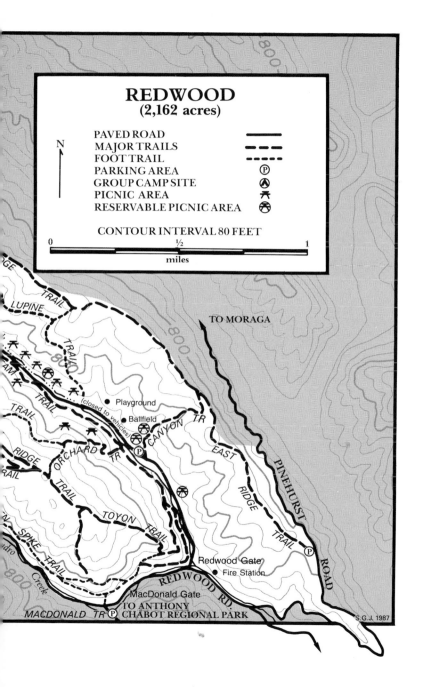

REDWOOD
(2,162 acres)

PAVED ROAD	——————
MAJOR TRAILS	– – – –
FOOT TRAIL	- - - - -
PARKING AREA	ⓟ
GROUP CAMP SITE	Ⓐ
PICNIC AREA	⚏
RESERVABLE PICNIC AREA	⊛

CONTOUR INTERVAL 80 FEET

0   ½   1
miles

N

800

800

TO MORAGA

LUPINE

TRAIL

TRAIL

80

TRAIL

(closed to vehicles)

● Playground

● Ballfield

CANYON TR

TR

ⓟ

EAST

RIDGE

PINEHURST

ORCHARD

TRAIL

TOYON TRAIL

RIDGE

TRAIL

ⓟ

SPIKE TRAIL

Creek

800

ROAD

Redwood Gate
● Fire Station

MacDonald Gate

REDWOOD RD.

MACDONALD TR ⓟ

TO ANTHONY
CHABOT REGIONAL PARK

S.G.J. 1987

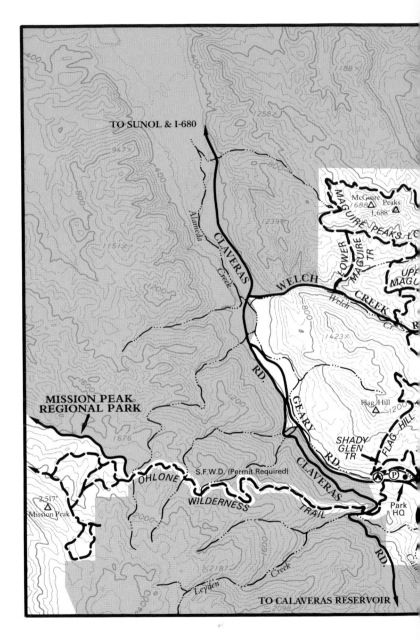

TO SUNOL & I-680

188

258

947

McGuire Peaks
1,688'

1239

1151

WELCH CREEK

Welch Cr

800

1423

Flag Hill
1200

FLAG HILL TR

MISSION PEAK
REGIONAL PARK

1576

GEARY RD.

SHADY GLEN TR

CLAVERAS RD.

S.F.W.D. (Permit Required)

OHLONE

WILDERNESS

TRAIL

Park HQ

2,517'
Mission Peak

2000

1600

2187

2098

Leyden Creek

TO CALAVERAS RESERVOIR

Map M

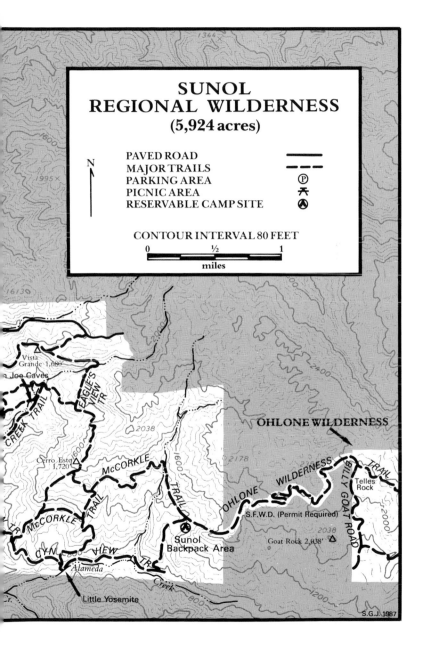

SUNOL
REGIONAL WILDERNESS
(5,924 acres)

N

PAVED ROAD	———
MAJOR TRAILS	– – –
PARKING AREA	Ⓟ
PICNIC AREA	𝝠
RESERVABLE CAMP SITE	Ⓐ

CONTOUR INTERVAL 80 FEET

0   ½   1

miles

OHLONE WILDERNESS

Vista Grande 1,680'

Joe Caves

CREEK TRAIL

EAGLE'S VIEW TR

Cerro Este 1,720'

McCORKLE TRAIL

OHLONE WILDERNESS

BILLY GOAT ROAD

TRAIL

Telles Rock

S.F.W.D. (Permit Required)

McCORKLE TRAIL

CYN VIEW TR

Alameda

Sunol Backpack Area

Goat Rock 2,038'

Creek

Little Yosemite

S.G.J. 1987

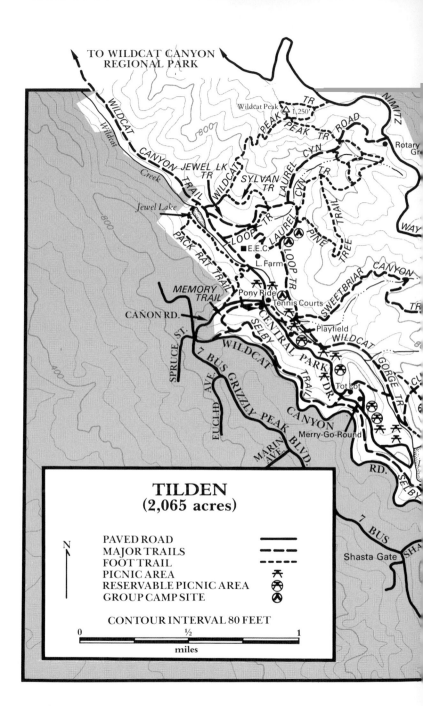

TO WILDCAT CANYON
REGIONAL PARK

Wildcat Peak △ 1,250'

Rotary Gr

NIMITZ

WAY

PEAK TR

PEAK TR

ROAD

WILDCAT CANYON TRAIL

Wildcat Creek

JEWEL LK TR

WILDCAT

SYLVAN TR

LAUREL CYN

CYN TR

PINE TREE TRAIL

Jewel Lake

PACK RAT TRAIL

LOOP TR

LAUREL

LOOP TR

E.E.C.

L. Farm

SWEETBRIAR CANYON TR

MEMORY TRAIL

CAÑON RD.

Pony Ride

Tennis Courts

Playfield

WILDCAT

SPRUCE ST.

7 BUS

WILDCAT

CENTRAL PARK DR.

SELBY

GORGE TR

EUCLID AVE.

GRIZZLY PEAK BLVD.

CANYON

Tot Lot

MARIN AVE.

Merry-Go-Round

RD.

SELBY

TILDEN
(2,065 acres)

N

PAVED ROAD	———
MAJOR TRAILS	– – –
FOOT TRAIL	- - -
PICNIC AREA	
RESERVABLE PICNIC AREA	
GROUP CAMP SITE	

7 BUS

Shasta Gate

SHA

CONTOUR INTERVAL 80 FEET

0   ½   1

miles

Map N

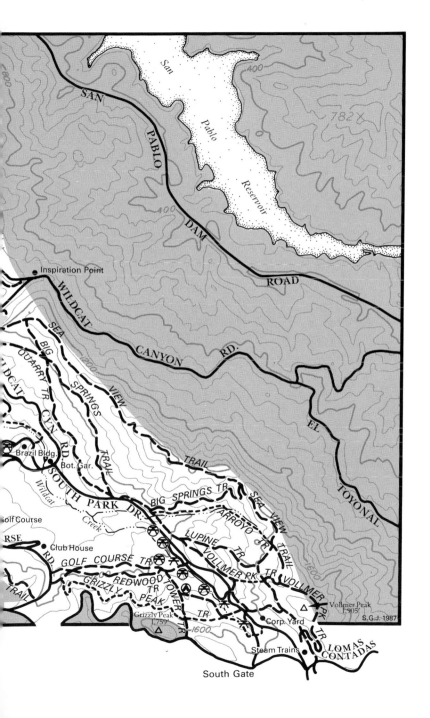

San Pablo Reservoir

SAN PABLO DAM ROAD

782 X

400

2800

400

Inspiration Point

WILDCAT CANYON RD.

SEA VIEW TRAIL

BIG SPRINGS TRAIL

EL TOYONAL

QUARRY TR

WILDCAT CYN. RD.

1200

Brazil Bldg.

Bot. Gar.

SOUTH PARK DR.

Wildcat Creek

BIG SPRINGS TR.

SEA VIEW TRAIL

ARROYO

Golf Course

Club House

RSE

RD.

GOLF COURSE TR.

LUPINE TR.

VOLLMER PK. TR.

VOLLMER PK. TR

1600

TRAIL

REDWOOD TR

GRIZZLY PEAK

Grizzly Peak 1,759

TR

1600

Corp. Yard

△ Vollmer Peak 1,905

S.G.J. 1987

Steam Trains

LOMAS CONTADAS

South Gate

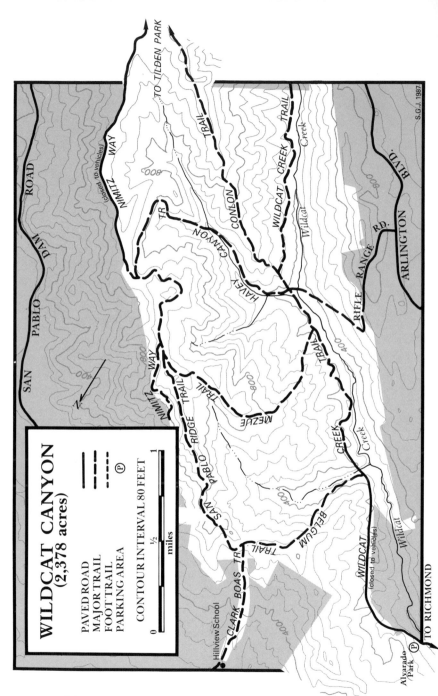

WILDCAT CANYON
(2,378 acres)

PAVED ROAD
MAJOR TRAIL
FOOT TRAIL
PARKING AREA   Ⓟ

CONTOUR INTERVAL 80 FEET

0   ½   1

miles

S.G.J. 1987

Map O

Lafayette–Moraga Trail

The Lafayette–Moraga Trail is a narrow, 7.5–mile ribbon of asphalt that follows Las Trampas Creek through the suburban fantasies of Lafayette and out into the more rural stretches of Moraga. At the Lafayette end of the trail, tall trees—walnuts, cypresses, pines, maples, weeping willows, and many others—spread deep, still pools of shade, cool even on the hottest days. From behind fences that screen spacious homes from sight, you hear sounds of Sunday barbecues and the splash of kids jumping into backyard swimming pools. From under the fences ivy and cultivated flowers creep to the edge of the trail, to mingle with mugwort, lupines, and other wild plants.

Toward Moraga the landscape changes, becoming less populated and more open. Soon you are passing through pear and walnut orchards, past meadows still grazed by livestock. The trail here is generally exposed and hot, more recognizably "Californian."

The original grading on the Lafayette–Moraga Trail was done by the Sacramento Northern Railroad Company, which laid track and began serving the area in 1913. Passenger and freight trains between Sacramento and Oakland would stop at the tiny hamlets of Concord, Walnut Creek, and Lafayette, then continue to Moraga, Canyon, and through a tunnel into Oakland. Service was discontinued by the railroad in the 1950s, and the right-of-way was abandoned. Only a few reminders of the railroad era remain, among them being the gentle grading of what is now the Lafayette–Moraga Trail, an occasional place name such as Reliez Station, and a habit that persists among older residents of the area of calling the Lafayette–Moraga Trail "The Tracks."

Being so close to houses, shopping centers, libraries, playgrounds, and schools, the Lafayette–Moraga Trail does not attract serious hikers. Instead, you will find here a very un-serious, but quite wonderful promenade of American suburbia. Elderly women walk their dogs; youngsters in white shorts bicycle to the tennis courts; young mothers push strollers; people of all ages saunter, amble, stride, or jog according to their ambitions or physical abilities. One of the tenderest sights (rare, I think, elsewhere) is the number of middle-aged and older couples who walk the trail holding hands. When people pass each other they smile and nod in a pleasant, neighborly fashion, fellow sojourners on a mysterious pilgrimage through the suburban dream.

The Lafayette–Moraga Trail is fundamentally an amenity to the people who live nearby. It reminds one of a country lane, an intimate place that connects to people's backyards, where they can move, talk, and smile at each other at a slower, more human pace. And although used primarily by the residents of the area, I feel that this trail could have a much greater impact—not so much as a place for others to visit, but as a model of what other communities might do with their deserted railroad rights-of-way.

Directions: To reach the northern end of the trail, take Highway 24 through the Caldecott Tunnel to Pleasant Hill Rd. Head south on Pleasant Hill Rd. to Olympic Blvd., and take a right. The trail entrance is at the intersection of Olympic Rd. and Reliez Station Rd.

To reach the southern end of the trail, take Highway 24 to the Orinda turnoff. Go right onto Moraga Way into Moraga. Turn right on Canyon Rd., and proceed to the Valle Vista Staging Area, which also serves as an entry into the hiking lands of East Bay Municipal Utility District.

CAMPING

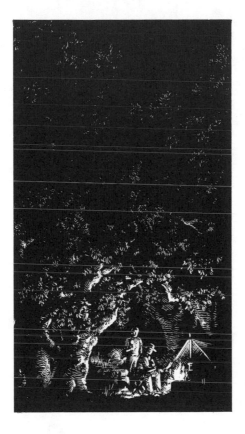

One day the people of Oakland discovered that someone had stolen night. The old folks remembered it dimly. Children's books still talked about it along with elves, kings, queens, trolls, and other bygone things. But no one remembered having seen a real night for many years.

Some people said it had been stolen by television. Others accused PG&E, the private automobile, the major oil companies, street lights, and the frantic pace of twentieth century living. At one point it was even rumored that night had never been stolen at all, but was lurking undiscovered in certain side streets and alleyways. Some of the braver citizens banded together for mutual protection and ventured out to verify the rumors. But instead of night all they found were a few paltry patches of darkness. Too bad, the old ones muttered: night has gone the way of the silent movies.

Cheer up, people of Oakland! I bring you good news. You can find plenty of night—pure, gorgeous, wholesome, sensuous night—at the East Bay Regional Park District campgrounds. There's so much night here that you can sleep in it, sniff it, listen to it, even roll in it. You can watch it creep out from among the late afternoon shadows, thicken between the hills, and drape itself delicately around the trees. It pushes nearby rocks and bushes into obscurity, while it draws the distant stars and moon close in upon us.

With a lantern or campfire you might, of course, hollow out a section of the night. With a flashlight you can punch a tunnel right through it. But when the night is big and healthy it will seal the holes and tunnels again without showing even the slightest scar. Night is not merely lack of day: it has sounds, smells, flowers, wildlife, a spirit, and an existence all its own.

The three family campgrounds run by the East Bay Regional Park District are Anthony Chabot in the Oakland Hills, Del Valle in the Livermore Hills, and Sunol near the town of Sunol. They are all close enough to encourage a spur-of-the-moment camping trip whenever you want to shake up your routine. For the more adventurous or mobile, Sunol Wilderness and Ohlone Wilderness have areas far from the nearest road set aside for back-country camping.

For new campers these various campgrounds offer the challenge of cooking over a fire (if you can get one going), sleeping on the lumpy ground, and washing burnt pots and pans in icy water. There is also the grateful discovery after your first night camping that you were not eaten by mountain lions, your tent was not trampled by cows, and your toes did not suffer from frostbite. For those of us who have mastered the basic expertise, there is satisfaction in the craftsmanship of camping, a sense of self-sufficiency and ease, and (best of all) a profound feeling of trust that if we give ourselves over to the land it will take good care of us and show us a good time. Which it will, indeed, at these East Bay Regional Park District campgrounds.

Chabot Campground

Anthony Chabot Family Campground is located twelve miles from downtown Oakland in Anthony Chabot Regional Park (page 20). The campground costs well over a half million dollars to build, but don't let that keep you away. The money doesn't show here. In fact, Chabot is a very simple, almost Spartan, campground. It has seventy-three sites arranged in clusters throughout an airy eucalyptus forest on the ridges above Lake Chabot. There's room for twelve trailers, and thirty-four of the sites are reserved for "walk-in" camping. There are flush toilets and hot showers.

I have had a very personal relationship with this campground. It brings back such vivid memories that I cannot see it freshly any more, the way you as a casual weekend camper might want it to be presented. When the campground first opened in 1972, I lived there in a tent for nearly three months as a semi-official caretaker. It was called Las Cumbres then, and the mere mention of the name brings back a flood of associations and memories: my son Reuben (then two years old) clad only in sneakers, running through the woods; my wife Rina pushing a wisp of hair out of her face as she hikes up the hill from Lake Chabot; the family of deer who came every evening to taste the delicacies of a newly planted lawn; the silvery glitter of millions of eucalyptus leaves shimmering like scimitars in the breeze; the roost tree behind the telephone booth at the entrance which contained the silent powerful presence of a red-tailed hawk; our twilight walks down to Lake Chabot which croaked with the voices of a thousand unseen frogs; the time we returned after a two-week vacation to find twenty-eight mice (we counted them!) living in our tent; the period of peacefulness, hope, and joy during the first part of our stay; our sadness as we watched the grass change from green to brown; the sense of isolation that crept in (almost unnoticed) when friends from the city visited us less and less frequently; the loneliness of Reuben without playmates; and (at last) the knowledge so painfully arrived at that camping is great for a month or two, but as a way of life it is not for us.

That was my experience camping at Chabot. Since, however, there is a fourteen-day limit, there's not much chance that you'll have the same experience I did. You will most likely find that Chabot is a very good place to camp for a short period of time. (It's also a very good place to put up visiting friends and relatives.) It is close to the major East Bay cities. The sites are pleasant, lightly shaded by eucalyptus trees, airy, relatively free of mosquitos and flies, and they offer splendid panoramic views of the surrounding countryside and Lake Chabot.

There is a lot of peacefulness at Chabot. In fact for some people there is an overdose of peacefulness. If you are looking for a quiet time away from things, Chabot is ideal. You can tie a hammock between two trees, grab a book you've been meaning to read for ages, stretch out on the

hammock, spread the book carefully over your belly, and fall asleep. Scenes like this abound at Chabot, where popular activities of the moment are napping, eating, and taking showers in the hot water shower stalls.

If, however, you want a more active time, you should bear in mind that entertainment is not going to jump out from behind the eucalyptus trees and seize you, but that you will have to go out and seek your own entertainment. Here are some ideas on where to go and what to do:

• Hike into the gentle, rolling, generous hills and meadows of Anthony Chabot Regional Park that surround the campground.

• Explore the eucalyptus environment.

• Hike down to Lake Chabot (about one-and-a-half hour round trip) for fishing, bird watching, frog watching, or simply watching your own reflections.

• For the kids you might consider bringing a plastic wading pool, badminton rackets, kites, horseshoes, and other appropriate toys.

• Visit these other Regional Parks that are within fifteen or twenty minutes of the campground: Cull Canyon, Don Castro, Redwood, and Lake Chabot.

• Or if on this camping trip you want to be rid of your car entirely, you can take an A.C. Transit bus (15A) to 11500 Skyline Boulevard (near the corner of Redwood Road), then backpack about eight or ten miles through Redwood Park and Anthony Chabot Park to the campground. For a shorter hike, you can take the 56A bus (on weekdays) to the corner of Golf Links Road and Grass Valley Road, and from there walk through Anthony Chabot Park to the campground. Although I have not done it myself, I find it very pleasing that someone can take a bus from Oakland to the city outskirts and then hike to a place as peaceful and away-from-it-all as Anthony Chabot Family Campground.

Directions: From Oakland or Berkeley, take Highway 13 (the Warren Freeway) to the Redwood Rd. exit. Go east (toward the hills) on Redwood Rd. past Skyline Blvd. and past the Redwood Regional Park entrance to Marcial Gate, and follow the signs from there. From the junction of Redwood Rd. and Skyline Blvd. to Marcial Gate is 8.3 miles.

Campsites may be reserved through Ticketron (see your phone book), although reservations are not generally needed.

See Map D.

Del Valle Campground

When you camp at Del Valle you don't seem to be inter-
rupting things very much by your presence. Even on hot
weekends—when all 150 sites are full and trailers come
floating through like luxury liners looking for a berth—
Del Valle seems to absorb its human visitors easily.

The campground is within walking distance of the lake
(see page 161). But it is hidden away in a broad flat valley.
This valley is the handiwork of the Arroyo del Valle
Creek, one of the major tributaries of Alameda Creek.
Arroyo del Valle is not one of those ambitious, upstart
little mountain creeks that rushes along, eager to make its
mark in the world by carving a deep, steep canyon. It
finished its carving and gouging many thousands of years
ago. Now it has slowed down to enjoy a leisurely old age,
as it meanders gently through the serene valley it created in
its wilder youth.

This is a fairly old valley, full of towering trees. Standing alongside the creek are the sycamores, chunky and
twisted, with almost frivolous pompom seeds. Massive
oaks spread out, expansive, like monarchs at a feast. The
digger pines are eccentric—seeming to defy gravity as
they strain off to one side.

In the branches jays hop and squawk at the earth-bound
campers below them. Raccoons and feral housecats plot
burglaries on garbage cans. But the acorn woodpeckers
scarcely acknowledge the tents and trailers as they carry on
their remarkable lives.

Acorn woodpeckers are handsome, swashbuckling birds
with black and white flecked bodies and red caps. They live
in colonies (actually communes) of about six to fifteen
birds. If you look among the sycamores in early May
you'll notice the youngsters crawling out of the nest. They
are at first wide-eyed, over-eager, and a bit clumsy, and
they are always under the watchful eye of an adult. Any

adult will do, since the whole colony shares equally in incubating the eggs, feeding and caring for the young, collecting food, and defending the territory.

The diet of the acorn woodpeckers is more varied than their name implies. You might see them feeding off the sap that exudes from tiny holes they have drilled into certain trees. In the spring and summer you'll see them perched on high branches from which they take long "hawking" flights after flying insects. But their most remarkable trait is the way they store acorns. They store food on a scale unequalled by any other bird. Their warehouses, or storage trees, are found throughout the campground, old giants of trees riddled with thousands of holes. Every year the woodpecker colony adds only two or three hundred new holes. So these old trees are like heirlooms, handed down and improved upon by many generations of this particular woodpecker colony.

Throughout the fall they work noisily yet efficiently, fitting acorns into the holes. The fit must be tight, as you are well aware if you try to remove an acorn. But the acorns tend to dry and shrink within their holes. The woodpeckers now scramble over the storage trees and rearrange their riches into smaller holes, like shopkeepers taking inventory of their stock. The same acorn may be moved as many as three times before it is finally eaten.

By mid-winter the crop is safely stored, and the colony can relax a little. At this time of year soft muffled hammerings fill the campground as the colony pecks out a few more holes to use next year and to pass along to future generations of woodpeckers.

For the kids, as well as for the woodpeckers, Del Valle is a hospitable environment. There are good climbing trees and other kids to play with, while the roads in the campground see a heavy traffic of bikes, trikes, and a variety of push 'em–pull 'em toys.

But the biggest attraction of all is the creek. Arroyo del Valle flows wide and full, often until mid-summer, and creates a series of natural pools—middle-sized pools for the middle-sized kids, smaller pools for the smaller kids, and little pee-warm pools for the very littlest kids. Even for adults there is no better way of spending a hot, fly-buzzy summer day than to sit among the rounded river rocks, splash in the pools, and look after butterflies and dragonflies as they flick and flutter among the creek willows, nestled and sheltered within the valley walls.

At night the gentle hammerings of the woodpeckers and the shouts of the kids are replaced by the hoots of owls, the piping of bats, and the chirps of insects. The gravelly voice of the creek seems louder now. I usually sleep in the open so I can listen to these night songs and engage in one of the oldest pursuits of our species—stargazing.

Even modern science has not stolen away the wonderment we feel toward the stars. If anything it has added to it. Modern telescopes, for example, have examined the bowl of the big dipper and discovered—no, not milk as in the old tale, but something more astonishing. In this one tiny area, black and empty to the naked eye, they have found literally millions of stars. In fact they have found whole galaxies, over 1,500 of them. Looking up at the stars, mulling over the inconceivable concept of light years, the meaning of infinity, and the possibilities presented by other galaxies, stretching the mind out over the whole expanse of the sky—this is the best way I know of sharpening our awareness of our basic condition: that we are tiny beings on the skin of an insignificant but oh, so lovely planet hurtling through vast, empty space.

Directions: From Oakland, take Highway 580 east to Livermore and exit at the North Livermore Ave. off ramp. Head south through town. North Livermore becomes South Livermore Ave., and eventually it veers east to become Tesla Rd. From Tesla Rd. turn right onto Mines Rd. After about three miles turn right again onto Del Valle Rd. which leads to the park entrance.

Reservations for campsites are advisable and may be made through Ticketron; consult your local phone book.

See Map F.

Sunol Campground

Every morning magpies pass through the Sunol campground to check out the garbage cans. They have yellow beaks, stunning black and white coats, and long iridescent tails. Their elegance is almost embarrassing. It's like having members of the Metropolitan Opera orchestra in full dress searching through your left-overs.

Except for the formality of the magpies, however, Sunol Family Campground is a casual, unpretentious place. There are only four official camp sites clustered together in an oak-bay forest on the banks of Alameda Creek. Above them (and out of sight) is a parking lot where trailers, pickup campers, and VW busses huddle together like covered wagons.

Sunol campground is often used as a launching pad for other activities. The hills around it provide exciting hiking (see page 72). For ten-speeders the campground is a good starting point for trips to the historic towns of Sunol, Niles, and Mission San Jose. But for most people Sunol campground is a place to lie back, toast a few marshmallows, and get acquainted with a fascinating forest and a noble creek.

At first glance the forest here is mostly oaks, bay trees, and a few streamside sycamores. But walk through the campground looking at the forest floor and you'll discover that almost all the young trees are bays. The evidence is very dramatic. In the not too distant future this forest will very probably become a pure bay forest.

This is not an unusual phenomenon. In many other hardwood forests—especially where there is cattle-grazing, heavy deer-browsing, or widespread people-trampling—you might notice a large percentage of bay saplings among the new growth. They survive and reproduce well on disturbed soil, and cattle and deer will eat almost anything else before they taste the strongly aromatic leaves of the bay tree. Forests change slowly, of course, and it will be a hundred years or more before we can be certain of this trend, but it seems likely that the bay tree is becoming the dominant tree of the East Bay.

But while forests change slowly, Alameda Creek has undergone very rapid transformations. The first Spanish explorers found the creek lined with sycamores and willows, looking very much like an arcade—or *alameda* in Spanish. This full, always-flowing creek so impressed itself upon the early settlers that they eventually named the county of Alameda after it.

But in recent years Alameda Creek has been shamefully degraded. Upstream, the San Francisco Water Department has built a dam to divert the water through a tunnel and into the Calaveras Reservoir. Downstream sections of the creek have been sentenced to life imprisonment within the stone and concrete channels of the Army Corps of Engineers. But at Sunol the creek is still pure and wild— and for those who know it well it is one of the most nourishing features of Alameda County.

In the spring the creek is thirty or forty feet wide and waist deep. It flows with steadiness, power, and determination not found in any other East Bay creek. Walk along its shores. A few hundred yards upstream from the campground the land spreads out into a broad valley where tall oaks and sycamores shade Sunol's main picnic areas, and where flowery meadows flow down to the banks of the creek. You lie back in the cool, green, springtime grass and watch as the creek catches the sun, dashes it to pieces, strains it out over the riffles, restores it whole in a quiet pool, and tosses it back at you with an unexpected glint.

About a mile past these green-grass, sunlit meadows along a pastoral country lane the valley turns into a steep canyon called "Little Yosemite." Here jumbles of rock and boulders break up the steady flow of the stream. The water rushes through this dark, steep gorge, dashing against the

rocks, splitting into hundreds of little waterfalls, and settling down to rest in dozens of calm pools. For those who can jump from rock to rock across the stream, Little Yosemite is an especially primitive and wild place.

During the summer the stream's flow diminishes. If (like most people) you limit your wildlife experiences to birds, deer, squirrels, and rabbits you might want to roll up your pants and wade out into the exotic environment of Alameda Creek. Among the creatures you will find are: waterstriders who perform the daily miracle of walking on water and whose shadows seem more real than their bodies; water scorpions; water boatsmen who row rapidly with their "oars"; turtles; frogs; whirligig beetles; the larvae of many familiar insects; and several kinds of fish, worms, and plants. This creek has prey, predators, and scavengers who make up a complete—and for most of us very little known—wildlife community.

For a different awareness of Alameda Creek you might try walking along its banks at night. Alameda Creek (like all streams) is blind, and at night one feels very close to it. Its night song is powerful, filling the air. And above the creek rise the jagged branches of trees like bolts of lightning against a starry sky.

At night you return to the campground and fall asleep listening to the deep, throaty murmurings of the creek. The river sounds flow through your mind and cleanse your consciousness. You awake in the morning to a cool dawn, a sparkling creek, and a flock of magpies. You awake onto a world that is fresh and newborn, a world of which you feel very much a part.

Directions: From Highway 680, exit at Calaveras Rd. in Sunol. Turn left (south) onto Calaveras Rd. to Geary Rd. The park entrance is at the end of Geary Rd.

For more information, a schedule of naturalist programs, or to reserve a campsite, call 862-2244.

See Map M.

HISTORY

 When I first began to explore the hills and shoreline of the East Bay in the early 1970s, I tended to value only the wild, the untouched, the aboriginal. I saw human history only as an intrusion upon the landscape. A hillside was for me somehow injured by the faint remains of an old foundation, a meadow scarred by the signs of an old paddock or fenceline. When I worked for the East Bay Regional Park District, leading youths on conservation projects between 1970 and 1972, my guiding principle was to remove the signs and influences of people—to erase history, in effect—and to return the land to its pristine state.

My fascination with the history of the East Bay has been a gradual, often reluctant, conversion. Yet a conversion it has been. At Mission Peak, for example, I now often pull myself away from a valley where I believe golden eagles are nesting to explore the squat stone walls built by unknown hands. At Wildcat Canyon I search out the crumbling, rose-covered ruins of old farm houses. I regularly visit apple orchards scattered throughout the hills whose bursts of white flowers each spring startle me into an awareness of otherwise forgotten homesteads and trustier human ways.

There is much history embedded in the East Bay landscape, but it speaks to us mostly in fragments of a foreign language—few of us even have one grandparent who was born in the East Bay—and generally in tantalizing whispers. We hear these whispers when we come upon a mortar hole or an arrowhead, pass through a valley named by earlier Spanish settlers, or stop to view the ghost-like tracing of an old skid road down which bygone loggers once snaked trees felled in a bygone forest. These whispers from the East Bay's past cause us to muse briefly. We are momentarily touched, thrown slightly off track, and then we pass on.

There are three East Bay Regional Parks, however, where history speaks with a fuller, stronger voice—a voice that can, at times, capture our attention, tell us a rich and complex story, draw us into the past. At Ardenwood Historic Farm we can wander through a Victorian house, help hitch a draft horse to a plow, churn butter, or spin wool. At Black Diamond Mines we can enter mine tunnels and explore the sites of mining towns that once dotted the northern slopes of Mount Diablo. And at Coyote Hills we can walk into a reconstructed Indian village and at certain times even sit under a shade house and practice the skills of the people who lived here for so many centuries before us. At Ardenwood, Black Diamond Mines, and Coyote Hills we can escape, not just the urban areas of the East Bay, but the twentieth century as well.

Ardenwood

When you first enter the 200-acre Ardenwood Historical Farm, you feel as if you have stepped into a movie set or perhaps a Currier and Ives lithograph. You pass by white picket fences and flower gardens of long-stemmed irises, then reach an expansive, well-trimmed, quite perfectly green lawn. Upon this large lawn you notice, among other things: a white gazebo; a peacock in grand display; a thin young man in suspenders chasing a hoop with a stick; and two women clad in Victorian ruffled dresses playing croquet. Before you stands a white gingerbread mansion with scalloped walls and tiffany windows. To think: you pulled off the freeway, took a sharp right turn, and five minutes later you have found yourself in the nineteenth century.

Or is it a picture-postcard fantasy of what the nineteenth century was supposed to have been like? This is not an easy question to answer, because there was a strong element of "picture-postcard" fantasy at Ardenwood even at its heyday in the late 1800s. It was named, in fact, after the forest in Shakespeare's *As You Like It,* where—among unpretentious shepherds and guileless swains—the good Duke and his retinue took refuge from the intrigues and evils of the court. Here they led lives of pastoral innocence, finding "tongues in trees, books in running brooks, sermons in stones, and good in everything." To Shakespeare's characters this forest represented a kind of Utopia, and I think the farm named after it represented a kind of Utopia to its original owners as well. As a glance at the resplendent peacock strutting across the lawn in front of the pure white gazebo would surely indicate, Ardenwood was never meant to be a humdrum, work-a-day farm.

In modern times the family farm has become for many an enslavement to poverty and a dawn-to-dusk struggle to keep up with the mortgage payments. In the nineteenth century, however, farming could still be a gentlemanly pursuit, a road to social prestige and great wealth—especially in the Fremont area. With its deep alluvial soils, its easy irrigation from Alameda Creek, its mild weather and long growing season, its relative lack of fog, and its convenient access to urban markets across the bay, Fremont was a "bread basket" for the entire Bay Area. Here George Patterson settled in 1851 to raise wheat, row crops, poultry, and cattle on a farm that would eventually cover six thousand acres of fertile land. Some of these goods were sold locally, but most were carted to Patterson's own landing at Coyote Hills, where his private boat transported the goods to San Francisco for sale. As his wealth increased, the house, originally built to more modest scale in 1856, was thoroughly remodelled in the 1880s. Patterson's wife, Clara Hawley—a well-educated woman, who was also a poet and a suffragette (Susan B. Anthony was a frequent house guest here)—saw to it that the house, with its private swimming pool, tennis court, and spacious grounds, would reflect the best in late Victorian taste.

"Welcome to the Patterson House," says the tour guide as visitors gather on the porch. "Mrs. Patterson isn't home right now, and she asked me to show you around," she continues, as if we were guests who had just arrived by wagon, and she—dressed in Victorian gown—were the maid. For the next hour she leads us from room to room, pointing out the flowery wallpaper, the gold-painted fringe of laurel leaves on the ceiling, the tiffany lamps, the curved windows, the decorative furnishings, the quilted bedspreads.

She pretends to be a maid, we pretend to be guests, and there are no red velvet ropes blocking off the rooms. Yet, despite her best efforts, I cannot help but feel that we are not in a real house, but in a museum. And I cannot help but wonder whether the members of the Patterson family themselves didn't also feel that they were living in a museum. This was not a house in which kids could run around, or in which one would even think of lying down on the living room couch for a nap. It seems too formal, too much like a dollhouse, too quaint and pretty. It reminds me of the way women were expected to look; a proper, upper-class Victorian woman wore some thirty pounds of clothing, her sleeves starched so stiffly that she could scarcely bend her arms, her corset pulled so tightly that she could hardly breathe. Women were dolls, fragile but visually delightful, so constrained by the garments they wore and the roles they played that they would have to resort continually to smelling salts to get through the day. It was a world that sacrificed comfort and sensuality for visual effect. I can imagine the delicate chinaware laid out for the afternoon tea. Others on the tour linger and seem to feel much at home here. I, however, leave quickly for the farmyard area.

It is with a decided feeling of relief that I enter the barn—a feeling which, although I was raised in the city, I can describe only as a "homecoming." The colors here are predominantly brown—wood, leather, sawdust, and earth—wonderfully deep, subtle, endlessly varied shades of brown. In the softened light even the air in the barn has a brown, well-used, familiar look to it. All around me are the sounds of an old-fashioned farm: the whinnying of horses, the hammering of a blacksmith, the clucking of chickens, the baaing of lambs. There is a mixture of animal and earthen smells, rich like compost, reminiscent of mushrooms, yet sweet. This is a world of balance and harmony, of utilitarian understatement and good sense. It is a place where everything has purpose and, to my eyes, deep beauty.

Plans call for this area to be set up eventually as a fully working, late nineteenth century farm. The blacksmith will make shoes for the draft horses. The draft horses will pull the combines to harvest the wheat. The wheat will be threshed in the granary, winnowed, ground into flour, and bread will be baked from the flour. The sheep in the pens

will be sheared, and their wool will be made into yarn on the spot. In short, what is planned is nothing less than a recreation of the nineteenth century itself.

Much of this is already taking shape. Activities vary, but on a given day you might find people making rope, quilting, making lace, spinning, weaving, canning or drying fruit, churning butter, having a square dance, caning a chair, and otherwise practicing crafts, now almost forgotten, that were once the common knowledge of virtually everyone in America. For visitors to Ardenwood there is an open invitation to join in. There are rides on horse-drawn wagons and a horse-drawn train, there are Victorian games to play, and skills to learn. Families that visit Ardenwood for a day's entertainment are well-occupied and well-rewarded.

But the illusion of the late nineteenth century is still far from complete. If Ardenwood is meant to be a theatrical performance, the stage setting is still under construction and the actors have not yet learned their lines perfectly.

I came across a woman, for example, dressed in a Victorian gown, who was making corn cakes on an antique griddle over an open fire. Beside her was a butter churn; passersby were asked to help churn the butter, and were then invited to taste the corn cakes. They were delicious, I must admit, but when I questioned her, the woman made a few confessions. Corn is grown, dried, decobbed, and ground into flour at Ardenwood, but the flour is too coarse for her tastes, so she is using store-bought corn meal. There is a rustic wicker basket full of farm eggs, but since the chickens at Ardenwood haven't been laying very well ("only two eggs yesterday") she bought the eggs at the local supermarket. Since there is no dairy herd yet, she also bought the cream that was put into the butter churn. "And I know I should be using molasses," she said defiantly, "but I hate the way molasses tastes, so I'm using sugar, instead."

Several years from now Ardenwood will probably be a much more polished enterprise, perhaps even a theme park that will offer a nicely-packaged educational experience. A competent staff will lead visitors on a smooth, faultless tour. It is, however, at the present time blessedly underdeveloped, and there is a clumsy, folksy quality to the place that I frankly enjoy. And I feel that while the technology might falter now and then, there is a freshness and pacing to Ardenwood now that accurately reflects a period when people had more time and were more neighborly, when men would putter around and women would chat while they quilted. For instance, in addition to a paid staff, docents, and volunteers, Ardenwood has visitors who come repeatedly and get involved. In many cases the visitors know more about old farming methods than the staff. "This is how we used to do it in Arkansas," an old man said one day, as he pushed a city-born naturalist aside, grabbed the reins of a draft horse, and plowed the straightest horse-drawn furrow that anyone in California has seen in fifty years. Another day someone showed up who knew how to harness thirty-two horses, rigged so that each horse would pull an exactly equal load—a feat prodigious to imagine, let alone execute. Men gather in groups to discuss the hub of a wagon wheel. One feels here that there are plenty of people to talk to and plenty of time, and an uncommon ease in striking up conversations. People who know are more than willing to share their knowledge. There is a peculiar quality of neighborliness here, recalling a time when getting to know your neighbor was a value and a possibility.

Ardenwood is a visit to the past. There is a possibility, however—and I mean this quite seriously—that it is also a visit to the future. It has been observed in many places back East that whereas technologically advanced family farms are in deep trouble, with massive bankruptcies and foreclosed mortgages, the Amish farmers—who for religious reasons still farm with draft horses, use manure, and forgo electricity and internal combustion engines—are prospering. They are prospering on relatively small acreages, materially as well as spiritually. Their dollar return per acre is much higher than that realized by their technologically more advanced (and addicted) neighbors. They do not work longer hours, and they enjoy their work far more. Farmer and writer Wendell Berry of Kentucky has been advocating the return to horse farming, and indeed the use of draft horses has been spreading dramatically throughout parts of the East.

If Ardenwood provides us not just with a look into the past, but also a look into the future, then judging from the social interchanges at the farm and barn it will be a tolerable future indeed. Perhaps Ardenwood is the forerunner of places where we will again "find tongues in trees, books in running brooks, sermons in stones, and good in everything."

Directions: To reach Ardenwood from the Nimitz Freeway (I-880), take the Decoto Rd./Dumbarton Bridge exit (Highway 84) west. Exit at Newark Blvd., and follow Newark Blvd./ Ardenwood Blvd. north to the park entrance.

For tour reservations or more information, call 796-0663.

Black Diamond Mines

As you enter Black Diamond Mines Regional Preserve along the narrow, twisting Somersville Road, you are greeted by one of the most exciting landscapes in the Bay Area. Unlike the typical East Bay hills—rounded, quiescent, apparently long retired from their youthful geological exertions—the hills of this 3,650-acre park appear jagged, chopped, and jumbled, their exposed rocky ridges and dramatic stone outcroppings suggesting an almost adolescent vigor. These rugged hills, covered mostly by grasslands, are splotched with stands of chaparral and with open, sun-lit groves of Coulter pine, digger pine, and blue oak. More arid than most of the East Bay, Black Diamond's ridges, peaks, and valleys remind me more of the Sierra foothills or the wildlands hundreds of miles to the south than they do of local scenery. The land seems expansive and untamed. You can hike for hours, visiting secluded side canyons or climbing the ridgetops for sweeping views. Out of sight of houses or paved roads, alone among the deer and the hawks, you might well imagine yourself to be far away from the effects of civilization.

At least it *feels* far away. But look more closely, and you will find an extraordinary human history imprinted on the land. The grassy hillsides are so deeply furrowed by cattle trails that they look like full-scale contour maps. The fading remains of old road cuts and railway beds are still impressed upon the grasslands. Scattered throughout the park, like huge gopher mounds, are heaps of naked rock and gravel—the tailings from dozens of abandoned mines.

Today it is almost impossible to think of the East Bay as coal mining country, but in the 1860s and 1870s this land was at the heart of the prosperous Mount Diablo Coal Fields. In valleys now grazed by cattle and browsed by deer, small mining towns once prospered. Mining companies employed hundreds of miners who, with picks and shovels, dug some 150 miles of tunnels into the hills. Three competing railroad lines built tracks into the area to haul the coal to Pittsburg Landing and New York Landing (three miles west of Pittsburg), where boats waited to transport the "black diamonds" to San Francisco and Stockton.

It is difficult to sit here under an open sky on a clear spring day, amidst bluebirds and flowering manzanita bushes, and recapture the misery of a nineteenth century coal miner. Of all the world's occupations, few were as degrading, brutalizing, or dangerous, particularly in an age before strong laws were passed or unions formed to offer miners even the most elementary protection. The veins of coal in the Mount Diablo Coal Fields were so narrow that the "rooms" and passageways in which miners worked were often no more than three feet high. Throughout the day a man might have to lie on his side to hack away at the walls of coal. The coal was then pushed along narrow passages; the floors of these passages often consisted of sheet iron greased with whale oil to allow the coal to slide more easily. When the coal reached the adits, or main tunnels, it was shoveled into railroad cars that generally had to be pushed by hand to the entrance.

In one of the mines was a workhorse that hadn't seen daylight for seven years. Humans were not treated much better. The air was thick with coal dust, the temperatures always cool, the tunnels dark, the measurable rates of injury and death very high, and the immeasurable rates of human misery even higher.

At the end of the day the miners would emerge from the tunnels, their faces covered with grime, their eyes squinting painfully even in the weak afternoon sunlight. It was an astoundingly different world into which they stepped—a world of flowering meadows and flourishing, mid-Victorian towns.

Nortonville and Somersville, the two major towns in the Mount Diablo Coal Fields, had populations of over five hundred people each by 1870, making them two of the largest towns in Contra Costa County. Smaller towns such as Stewartsville, West Hartley, and Judsonville also thrived. It is amazing to consider how much commercial and social activity small towns such as these once sustained. Nortonville of 1870 had three general merchandise stores (a fourth was then under construction), three hotels, four boarding houses, six saloons, and a livery stable. Somersville supported four general stores, one drug store, one hotel, two large boarding houses and several smaller ones, one doctor, one barber, a shoemaker, and four saloons.

Even more amazing is the fact that at the end of a twelve-hour work day, the coal miners still had time and energy to socialize. But they did. Among the fraternal organizations at Nortonville were branches of the Good Templars, Knights of Pythias, and Odd Fellows. Nortonville also boasted two Welsh literary societies (many of the coal miners came from Wales), a "Social Club" for the improvement and entertainment of its members, a Dramatic Society, a Baseball Club that fielded the best team in the region, a Glee Club that won praise from San Francisco critics, and a brass band that gave frequent concerts, played at balls, and headed every parade. So keen were the desires of this largely immigrant community for self-improvement, that Nortonville had one of the best public schools in the county and also supported a night school "for the benefit of the young men who labor in the mines during school hours."

In the mid-1880s, improvements in transportation and mining techniques suddenly brought large quantities of inexpensive, high-grade coal into the Bay Area from foreign countries and from newly opened coal fields in Oregon and Washington. In a few short years, mining activity in the Mount Diablo Coal Fields virtually ceased, and the once bustling towns were deserted. An article in the *Contra Costa Gazette,* October 10, 1885, described the plight of Nortonville.

It is sad to visit a town in the throes of dissolution that so short a time ago was so proud and prosperous as Nortonville was. . . . The few inhabitants still remaining are hopelessly stranded, with no possibility of relief, else they too would leave. Unfortunately the sturdy miners must leave substantial houses and beautiful homes behind them. Some of the more fortunate, who have snatched a few dimes from Dame Fortune are able to wash the grime and coal dust from their faces, take their houses to pieces, move to better places and rebuild and yet it is sad to witness this decay and dissolution of a town once so proud and prosperous.

For the next several years a few mines continued marginal operations, but by 1902 the last of them sealed its doors. In the end nearly four million tons of coal had been removed. It is thought that over seven million tons of coal are still in the ground.

By the 1920s this area of ghost towns saw a second mining boom, this time for silica sand, which was needed for local glassmaking and casting. New miners came into the area to hollow out large rooms as they removed some 1,500,000 tons of sand. The sand mines operated until 1949, when imported material and the closing of local industry caused an end to all commercial mining activity in the Black Diamond Mines area.

For the next twenty-five years the area was totally deserted. Buildings that had not been moved, decayed and were burned by vandals. The land was returned to grazing. The only visitors were local youngsters who came to explore the miles of dangerous, deserted mine tunnels—sometimes with fatal results.

In 1974 the East Bay Regional Park District acquired the land. To render the area safe, it sealed most of the mine adits and shafts, leaving just a few of the smaller and safer ones open for public exploration. One of the larger tunnels was restored, and the Park District offers highly popular weekend tours through the underground chambers.

Much of the Park District's interpretive effort at Black Diamond Mines has been focused on the mining history of the area. But if there had never been any mining, the vigorous topography, the unusual vegetation, and the spacious feeling of the land would still make this one of the most intriguing of the East Bay Regional Parks.

Despite its history, Black Diamond Mines is exciting, wild land. A gentle but insistent wildness has almost completely absorbed the old mining towns, covering their sites with a profusion of grasses and wildflowers, repopulating their streets and alleyways with wildlife. On various trips to Black Diamond Mines I have heard coyotes howl at dusk, watched golden eagles soar, surprised rattlesnakes sunning themselves on the trail, followed the flight of a prairie falcon, and stumbled upon what I am fairly certain were mountain lion signs.

A land such as this can easily absorb the attention and cares of anyone who comes here. There are long, leisurely hikes in the high meadowlands and broad valleys to the east. (For a particularly rewarding hike you can walk to Contra Loma Regional Park—see page 154—and treat yourself to a well-earned swim before heading back.) The trails to the west follow ridgetops from which you can view valleys so apparently pristine and beautiful that you are afraid to enter them lest they prove to be mere mirages.

While at Black Diamond Mines there are a number of unusual plants you might look out for. In the chaparral community (most readily accessible by the Chaparral Loop Trail, not far from the main parking area), you can find black sage, pitcher sage, coyote mint, Fremont globe mallow, bush poppy, mountain mahogany, and a variety of other shrubs and flowers. Most people, I suspect, find these chaparral slopes most inviting in the spring, when the leaves are fresh, the flowers blooming, and the air is cool. But I personally feel myself drawn to this area in the summer when the intense sun beats down upon the chaparral. The leaves exude sweet, spicy, intimate breaths. On windless afternoons the breaths of the various plants accumulate in deep pools, their scents so complexly mingled

and thick that I keep thinking that if I were to cut a chunk out of the air with a knife, I could carry the smell around with me forever.

The blue oak, a tree of the hot Sierra foothills, also seems quite at home in the heat of summer. It has gnarled branches and small, lobed, leathery leaves. Throughout the summer it has a bluish cast that gives the tree its name and the hillsides their distinctive, hazy coloration. I thought I knew the tree very well, until one day in April when it came out with a display of flowers so brightly— almost garishly—green that I was shocked: embarrassed and at the same time delighted that my old, blue friend would behave with such unexpected frivolity.

Noteworthy, too, are the two species of pine found here. The Coulter pine is also called the big-cone pine; its cones can be as long as eighteen inches and weigh up to eight pounds. Closely associated with the mountains and foothills of Southern California, Black Diamond Mines representing the northern limit of its range.

The second species of pine, the digger pine, also has large cones, though not as outlandishly large as those of the Coulter. Its long needles have a characteristically smoky, grayish coloring. The most remarkable feature of this tree, however, is its seeming transparency. So sparse is the foliage, so light gray, that you seem to be able to see straight through it, and it casts almost no shadow at all— more like a ghost than a real tree.

Ah, ghosts! Is this why, after a long day's hike at Black Diamond Mines, I often pause for a few minutes at the Rose Hill Cemetery to wander among the nineteenth century gravestones and pay my respects to the Welsh coal miners and their families buried here? How young these people were when they died, and how meticulously they tallied their brief time alive!

- Rebecca, beloved wife of John Evans, died at age 33 years, 1 month, 23 days;

- Mrs. Maggie Buxton, died at age 40 years, 2 months, 27 days;
- Katie, daughter of J. & B. Aitken, died December 24, 1879, age 8 years, 4 months, 12 days;
- Barbara, wife of W.B. Witheroy, died on August 7, 1876, aged 18 years, 2 months, 10 days.

Nowadays, Black Diamond Mines is a place set aside for beauty. The soft beauty of a spring landscape, fresh and newly born, is obvious to everyone who visits here. The beauty of a bluebird perched on a fencepost amidst the dry meadow grasses of summer is likewise obvious. But also to be appreciated is the beauty of the Welsh coal miners and their families who once lived here. Their baseball team, I can't help but remember, was "one of the best in the region." Their drama society, their night school, and their literary societies thrived. Their glee club was praised even by the San Francisco critics. And—just imagine—in those times of hard work and shortened lives, they even had the exuberance for a brass band!

Directions: From Highway 4, take the Somersville Rd. exit near Antioch. Head south on Somersville Rd. to the park entrance.
To make reservations for a mine tour, call 757-2620.
See Map B.

Coyote Hills

In the spring of 1769 Gaspar de Portolá led the first land expedition from Mexico into California. The small band of sixty-three men trudged along the ocean coast, climbing endless numbers of hills and struggling across countless steep-banked creeks. On November 1st, three-and-a-half months after they left San Diego Bay, they were exhausted, hungry, confused, and fighting among themselves. They passed Half Moon Bay, climbed over Montara Peak, and came to a halt at a small Indian village named Pruristac, near present-day Pacifica.

The next day, November 2nd, Portolá dispatched a party of soldiers into the hills to hunt for deer. I picture them now, a small group of soldiers, climbing steadily up the grassy slopes and through the oak woodlands, until they reached the summit. Here they stopped, astounded. Spread out before them, unexpected and undreamed of, was the San Francisco Bay in all its beauty. "*Un imenso brazo de mar*," they called it—an immense arm of the sea.

I think of that moment often, picturing the Bay as it must have been on that fateful day. Hundreds of square miles of saltwater marshland, drained and fed by an intricate nerve system of channels, shimmered in the afternoon sun. Herds of pronghorn antelope and tule elk grazed on the grassy plains of the East Bay shoreline. Lofty sycamores and cottonwoods lined Alameda Creek, and the great savannah of the Santa Clara Valley, dotted with oaks, extended southward into the haze as far as the eye could see. Strings of ducks and geese flew through the air, forerunners of the huge flocks that would soon arrive to darken the sky with their numbers. And everywhere the soldiers looked—so they reported to Portolá later that day—columns of smoke spiralled into the air from the

Indian villages below. The area, they concluded, must have been very well populated.

Near the mouth of Alameda Creek, partially sheltered from the winds of the Bay by a low-lying range of hills, was an Indian village that probably consisted of a dozen or so dome-shaped tule houses. Surely the people of that village—an Ohlone group who spoke a language called Chochenyo and who called themselves the Tuibun—had no idea that they were being watched on November 2, 1769. I imagine that the village would have been largely deserted that day. Most of the people would have been camping in the oak groves further inland, preparing for the acorn harvest. Only a few older people would have been left behind. Perhaps the smoke seen by the soldiers that day was spiralling out of sweathouses along the edge of Alameda Creek, where a few of the older men might have withdrawn, in part to keep warm, in part to repair the sacred feather capes and headdresses for the winter ceremonies that would follow the acorn harvest.

Today the village site, identified by partially excavated shellmounds (or middens), has been fenced off. Part of the 1,000-acre Coyote Hills Regional Park, it is the home of an extraordinary living history program. Naturalists, with the help of volunteers, have reconstructed some of the Indian buildings—tule houses, a subterranean sweathouse, a dance house, a shade house, and a dance pit. Here people get together to discuss Indian ways, and hands skilled at typewriters and computers have been learning the far more difficult arts of twisting string out of milkweed fiber, chipping arrowheads out of flint or obsidian, and coaxing fire out of wooden fire sticks. Games are played, songs sung, and stories told as close as possible to those of Indian times. Once a year naturalists and a crew of volunteers wade out into the marshes to collect tule and construct an Ohlone-style boat, which they paddle out into the Bay. Drop by and visit this village soon, and enroll in one of the "old ways" workshops. Sitting crosslegged on a tule mat beneath the roof of a shade house, you may find that you are not just chipping away at a piece of obsidian, but at the hard coat of twentieth century attitudes and values as well.

The reconstructed village is only a small part of Coyote Hills Regional Park. The hills that give the park its name are a Lilliputian mountain range rising only two or three hundred feet high. The rest of the park is a flat patchwork of saltwater marshes, mudflats, salt ponds, freshwater marshes, and meadows.

It is for good reason that this area once supported one of the densest Indian populations in all North America. The animal life was abundant beyond belief. And—while the antelope, elk, and grizzly bears are gone—the wildlife still is abundant. Saltwater marshes, of which there is still a remnant, provide what is reputed to be the richest wildlife environment in North America. The salt evaporating ponds that have replaced much of the marshland still attract legions of gulls, avocets, and stilts that feed on brine shrimp and on other creatures of these warm, shallow waters. Sandpipers race over the mudflats, while egrets and herons tiptoe through the water.

On the grasslands and hillsides, phoebes, swallows, shrikes, and flocks of well-tailored meadow larks harvest the fringes of the vast insect population. Red-tailed hawks sweep low over the hills and meadows, looking for ground squirrels, gophers, snakes, mice, or jack rabbits that thrive in the tall grass.

In the freshwater marshes, common blackbirds, red-winged blackbirds, and the relatively uncommon tricolored blackbirds all flock and bustle. Overhead fly the rare white-tailed kites and marsh hawks. Frogs croak throughout the marsh.

Muskrats play a very important part in the marsh ecology. If it weren't for them these shallow waters would quickly choke up with cattails and tules. For-

tunately, the muskrats have a good appetite for roots. They keep the ponds and passageways clear, and their dens rise like pyramids in the patches of blue water.

In late fall the most spectacular show of all begins, as the marshes swell with the first rains and the massive flocks of ducks arrive from Alaska and Canada. Some flocks are so large you can hear the whirring of their wings as they fly overhead. These are not tame ducks you can bribe with a piece of stale bread. They are wild ducks, wary of hunters and worldly-wise. You can't get too close, so bring binoculars and sit back somewhere to enjoy one of the greatest duck shows anywhere. Some ducks sit high in the water and move with princelike effortlessness. Others sit low in the water and seem to be fighting, kicking, and pumping hard just to move a few inches. Diving ducks slip easily beneath the water, scarcely rippling the surface as they disappear from sight. In contrast, dabblers thrust only their necks and heads under water, leaving their behinds waggling in the air. In spring the great flocks become restless and head north again, leaving behind them a smaller number of resident ducks to nest and raise their young in the shrinking waters of the marsh.

How did such a remarkable land escape the typical fate of development? Coyote Hills, part of the enormous Patterson Ranch, remained in the Patterson family from 1852 through 1968. A narrow gauge train plying the Newark–San Jose route once ran nearby, and as its whistles wailed across the plains, coyotes living in these hills would howl in reply. In the present century the area became the scene of an exclusive duck hunting club formed by Patterson along with members of the Bohemian Club. The land was stocked with pheasants, and even today as you hike through the brush and thickets you occasionally flush one of these glowing, handsome birds.

Since 1968 Coyote Hills has belonged to the East Bay Regional Park District. What does the future hold for this varied but fragile environment in the midst of a rapidly growing part of the Bay Area? Despite large-scale tract home developments that are moving in from the east, there is reason to be optimistic. Coyote Hills, while still managed by the East Bay Regional Park District, now falls within the boundaries of the San Francisco Bay National Wildlife Refuge. The refuge, covering 23,000 acres of salt ponds, marshes, and mudflats, offers hope that we will be able to manage the southern part of the Bay so that the rich bird population will not be just a historical memory, but a present (and future) reality as well. And, in preserving the environment, we will also be preserving a sense of what the land was like in those long gone days when smoke spiralled up from the villages of one of the densest Indian populations in all North America.

Directions: Take the Nimitz Freeway (Highway 880) to the Decoto Rd./Route 84 exit in Fremont. Head west on Highway 84 to the Thornton Ave./Paseo Padre Parkway exit, then head north on Paseo Padre for about a mile to Patterson Ranch Rd./ Commerce. Turn left on Patterson Ranch Rd. to the park entrance.
   For information on tours and activities, call 795-9385.
   See Map E.

Appendix

I shudder to think what the East Bay would be like if it were not for the East Bay Regional Park District. Homes, roads, and telephone poles would have spread from the cities over the hills. Tilden, Redwood, Sunol, and most of our finest parkland would probably be covered by tract home developments. Lakes like Chabot, Don Castro, and Contra Loma might still be fenced off, and virtually all public swimming would take place in tiled urban pools with their chain-link environments and chlorine smells. Anyone wanting to get away from it all would have to undertake a long, often exasperating drive to the State and National Parks outside our area. Without the East Bay Regional Park District we would live in a more crowded, ugly, vastly impoverished area—if we cared to live here at all.

As early as the nineteenth century a few visionaries (like Frederick Law Olmsted, architect of New York's Central Park) had suggested that the Oakland–Berkeley Hills be set aside as a natural area. But in those days the whole East Bay was by and large a "natural area" of wooded canyons and rolling pastures, and no one felt the need to put aside any land.

The impetus to create a park district came in the 1920s when the East Bay Municipal Utilities District (EBMUD) was formed to build a pipeline from the Sierra and consolidate the operations of several small independent water companies that were then serving the East Bay. As part of its "dowry," EBMUD received 40,000 acres of watershed land in the East Bay Hills. It felt, however, that it needed only 30,000 acres, and the remaining 10,000 acres (including what is now Tilden, Sibley, and Redwood Regional Parks) were declared surplus and up for sale. The automobile had made this rugged back-country accessible, and conservationists—afraid that the lands would be lost to developers—caused the formation of a special governmental district, the East Bay Regional Park District, to buy these surplus lands and manage them as parks. The first purchases took place in the mid-1930s. The Park District lawyer who negotiated them was Earl Warren, later governor of California and chief justice of the U.S. Supreme Court.

Since then the Park District has grown to include more than 60,000 acres of land distributed among more than forty parks. The citizens within its boundaries (most of Contra Costa and Alameda counties) support the Park District by paying an assessment on their property tax.

The East Bay Regional Park District is now more than fifty years old, and it has been of tremendous benefit to the people, plants, and wildlife of the East Bay. We can hardly do without it. But like any other middle-aged public bureaucracy, the East Bay Regional Park District desperately needs public involvement. At stake are such issues as whether future land acquisitions should include more recreation areas, more pocket picnic areas, more city-oriented parks, or more semi-wilderness areas. What kind of development should be encouraged? Should there be more horse trails or more hiking trails? More public campgrounds? More concession stands? These are some of the questions that are constantly being debated, often with inadequate public input. The management and staff are "public servants," but in truth they are seldom approached by the public they theoretically serve. The Board meetings are open to all, but few attend. Hundreds of thousands of people visit the parks each year, but only a handful ever write or telephone to express their opinions. Within the last four years you helped elect a member of the Board of Directors: do you remember whom you voted for, what your candidate stood for, or what your candidate's voting record has been since he or she was elected? As long as we all think that things will take care of themselves, the Park

District is bound to rest on its past accomplishments, become less and less responsive to our needs, and ultimately decay.

We all need a strong, sensitive, visionary East Bay Regional Park District. And the only way to make it strong, sensitive, and visionary is to feed it as much criticism, praise, energy, and involvement as each of us can afford.

As a minimum, at least keep informed. Although the parks are, of course, open to everyone, a Park District membership will get you the *Regional Parks Log,* a monthly newsletter of activities and developments in the regional parks, plus other benefits and privileges. If you have more time and energy, you might inquire about serving on an advisory committee.

For more information on joining the Regional Parks, or to find out about committees, public hearings, or board meetings, contact the Public Affairs Department, East Bay Regional Park District, 11500 Skyline Blvd., Oakland, CA 94619. The phone number is (415) 531–9300.

MALCOLM MARGOLIN grew up in Boston, Massachusetts. He worked for the East Bay Regional Park District for three years in the early 1970s, running youth conservation projects at Redwood Regional Park. He has written three other books and numerous articles, mostly on natural history, California Indians, and publishing. He is the owner of Heyday Books in Berkeley, and is publisher and co-editor of *News from Native California,* a bimonthly periodical devoted to California Indians.

CARL DENNIS BUELL was born and raised in rural upstate New York. He was the natural history illustrator at the New York State Museum, and his drawings and paintings have appeared in books and magazines nationwide. He currently works as a freelance natural science illustrator in San Francisco and lives along the borders of Anthony Chabot Regional Park.

SHARON G. JOHNSON, who hails originally from Santa Barbara, is a geographer. In addition to doing freelance cartography and land use consulting, she teaches in the geography department at San Francisco State University and often leads field trips to California's mountains, deserts, and rivers.